Book of Gemstones

(Gems their Occult & Remedial Powers)

Book of Gemstones

(Gems their Occult & Remedial Powers)

BIPUL PATHAK

Sagar Publications

72, Janpath, Ved Mansion
New Delhi-110001
E-mail: sagarpub@del3.vsnl.net.in
Tel.: 23320648, 23328245

First edition, 2005

Published and printed by Saurabh Sagar for Sagar Publications New Delhi-110001 and printed at The Artwaves, Y-56, Okhla Industrial Area, Phase-II, New Delhi-20, E-mail: theartwaves@rediffmail.com.

Dedicated To

My beloved wife Rupa

For all the support she has rendered to me over the years.

Acknowledgment

The present book has been a result of encouragement provided by Dr. Prem Kumar Sharma. My association with him and his guidance brought out the writer in me. I am grateful to Dr. Sharma who inspired me to write this book.

The book is original in many aspects but contains material, which is standard in the field of astrology and study of gemstones. I wish to acknowledge all those authors of books, periodicals, and articles, which I studied over a period of 5 years before practicing prescription of gemstones. I have used material from various other sources and wish to acknowledge that as well.

I wish to acknowledge my friends, batch mates and colleagues in my service, who allowed me initially to take liberty with their horoscopes and prescribe them gemstones. Later, they allowed me to use their horoscopes in the book. These details have given a unique character to the book as most of the chapters contain horoscopes of ordinary but successful people. This shows the human frailty that even successful people have problems just like the ordinary and not so successful people.

The contribution of my wife Rupa in allowing me to encroach her time for pursuing Astrology is invaluable.

Bipul Pathak
New Delhi
1st Nov 2005

Preface

Gemstones are an integral part of remedial measures used in Astrology. Gemologists study gemstones from a different point of view, but astrologers prescribe them for entirely different reasons. The book attempts to put both the areas in a holistic manner.

The purpose of writing this book was to bring these scientific aspects of the study of gemstones into focus. The chemical composition and the effects of various gemstones will arouse the reader with a scientific temper to read the subject in more details and the book will also take him into the realm of Astrology.

It is felt that, the details of prescription of gemstones and various techniques, will make a reader get attracted towards the fascinating science of Astrology as well. For others, the book can be a guiding factor for using appropriate gemstones. The book is equally useful for persons with the knowledge of Astrology, as they can easily understand the technical details discussed in various examples and case studies.

The book requires some basic knowledge of astrology for its full comprehension. Thus, for some readers, the book may serve as an initiator of interest in Astrology.

I have attempted to include most of the aspects of the subject in the book, yet I know it is not complete. I may enlarge it a later date. I would be very happy to receive suggestions from the readers for improving and enlarging the book.

Bipul Pathak
pathak_bipul@yahoo.com

Contents

Chapter 1

Introduction to Gemstones

Gemstones, over the years have been seen as representing wealth and power. Symbols of supremacy like crowns and richly decorated clothes and robes have traditionally been adorned with jewels. But gemstones are not just for the wealthy or scientifically minded researcher. But these can be appreciated by common man also just to enjoy the beauty of these gems. The gemstones appeal initially due to their mysterious appeal, lustre and their colour. This makes them exquisite but their rarity, hardness and durability makes them doubly valuable.

The ornamental use of gemstones is the first thing, which a man understands in life. One can see these gemstones being used for jewellery making and even the kings and queens of past had them. Many such precious stones have led to invasions of territories in the past, as these were valuable pieces. In addition to these ornamental uses, many civilisations have been using these gemstones for their healing and therapeutic use as well. Tibetan system uses it since very olden times. In the Indian context also, we find that these were used by astrologers for prescribing them for certain specific purposes. In ancient times, it was only the nobility and kings who could afford to use them and the astrologers also kept their use limited to this class of people. But with the advent of machines and modern mining techniques, their availability has increased and it has come well within the grasp of common man both for ornamental as well as healing purpose. The ancients knew their uses and we find that the deities associated with various planets in astrology have a specific gemstone adorned on that deity signifying the connection of astrology, planets and the gemstones.

Gemstones are basically minerals. Out of a total of more than 2500 different minerals, only about 60 odd are commonly used as gemstones. Other minerals are unsuitable as gems because they are too soft and get scratched easily.

A mineral (or occasionally an organic mineral) to be called a gemstone, it must be beautiful in its appearance and colour. A gemstone has to be durable-i.e. It should be hard enough to survive constant use and handling without getting scratched or damaged. Finally, it must be rare, because its scarcity makes it valuable.

Types of Gemstones

Mineral Gemstones:

Gemstones that are of mineral origin are found in rocks, or in gem gravels derived from these rocks. Rocks themselves are made up of one or more minerals. The formation of these rocks is a continuous and ongoing process. Gem quality minerals within these rocks may be easily accessible at the earth's surface or they can lie buried deep inside it. Sometimes these gem laden rock gravels get separated from their host rock due to erosion and are carried long distances by rivers to lakes, sea and shallow areas.

In Igneous rocks, which form due to solidification from the molten rocks, many gemstones are found. Some igneous rocks are extrusive where it solidifies after volcanic eruption and some are intrusive rocks where it solidifies beneath the earth. The rate of solidification determines the size of crystals found. Slower the rate, larger the crystal and consequently larger the size of gemstones in it.

In case of Sedimentary rocks, which are normally found in layers, sometimes the gems found here also show these layers in them.

Metamorphic rocks are either Igneous or Sedimentary, which have changed beneath the earth due to heat and pressure and has resulted in new form of minerals in it. During this process gemstones also grow within them. Some of the gems found in these rocks show mixed characteristics in their crystal structure, which provides hints about the basic rock formation, which has metamorphosed into the present state of Gemstone.

Organic Gemstones:

Organic gemstones have their origin either from plants or from animal sources. Like natural Pearls form around foreign bodies that have made their way inside the shells of marine or freshwater shellfish. These marine fish produce a fluid around the foreign body to protect themselves. This fluid solidifies and the fish continues to produce the fluid. This way layers after layers are formed around the foreign body and ultimately the pearl is formed. The more time is given, the bigger is the size of the pearl. Moreover, the size of the foreign body also decides the size of pearl ultimately. The type of fish can decide about the colour of pearls. We find grey, orange and white pearls in the market. Cultured pearls are produced artificially in large fisheries, many in the shallow waters off the seashores. The technique remains the same, except that the foreign body is inserted inside the shellfish. This way mass production of Pearls is done.

Shells, which are regarded as gems, may come from animals as diverse as snails and turtles, living in the ocean, in fresh water or on land. Coral is made up of the skeletons of tiny marine animals called Coral Polyps. These animals live in shallow seawater and feed on the seaweed to survive. They live in colonies and when they die, they leave behind their skeletal remains. Over the years they form into a huge coral reef.

Amber is fossilized tree resin, collected from soft sediments or the sea. Jet is fossilized wood, found in some sedimentary rocks.

Synthetic Gemstones:

Synthetic gemstones are made in laboratories or factories, not in rocks. They virtually have the same chemical composition and crystal structure as natural gemstones and consequently their optical and physical properties are very similar. However, they can usually be identified by the difference in the inclusions in them. Many types of gems have been synthesized but only a few are produced commercially, generally for scientific or industrial use.

Because of the way the synthetic gems are made, they show subtle differences in shape and colour that help to distinguish them from their natural counterparts. Similarly, the synthetic gems have inclusions, which are different from the natural inclusions. The experts can identify them and distinguish.

Gems are scientifically fascinating too. Gemmologists make a complete study of each stone, both as it is found in the rocks and after it has been cut and polished. That is why during the formal study of gems, both aspects are given due importance. This makes gemmologists distinguish between two similar looking stones, one of which may be fake. The science of gemmology looks at these minerals by way of their crystal structure and the physical properties. Everybody interested in buying gems (for whatever purpose) should have an idea of these properties.

Hardness

One of the key qualities of a gemstone is hardness. This means how well a gemstone resists scratching. Higher the hardness, more durable is the stone. Diamond is the hardest gemstone known and has been assigned hardness of 10 on Moh's scale of hardness. The Talc has been given lowest hardness of 1 on this scale. All gemstones are rated on a scale of 1 to 10.

Specific Gravity

This property shows the density of the gem. In common parlance it shows the heaviness of the gem. The greater the specific gravity, the heavier the gem will feel. Specific gravity of some of the stones is such that their size belies their weight. Thus, it becomes very easy to identify those gems.

Crystal Structure

This gives a definite clue about the gem's internal structure and is used by experts to differentiate between fakes and original gems. The crystal structure also helps in cutting and polishing the gems to give them shapes in which they look most beautiful.

Optical Properties

These properties are also used by researchers and experts to differentiate and decide about the ways of cutting and polishing the gems. Various optical properties are useful in gem therapy also as these properties help in harnessing the gem's full potential for healing purposes.

Chapter 2

Astrology and Gemstones

History of Gemstones:

Ancient Roman writer Pliny (62-113 AD) had written that there was a very large market for jewels and precious stones on the Secundra port in Egypt. Merchants, traders from Rome, Athens and other parts of the world used to come with their merchandise here. Jewels and precious stones with all their powers were mentioned even before these centres came into existence in Holy Bible and even before that in Vishnu Puran.

Who has not read about the great hall in which beautiful empress Cleopatra had received the Roman Emperor Julius Caesar, which was decorated with furniture studded with rare gems and Jewels. In recent history, the Peacock throne of the Moghuls was studded with jewels of all kind and had attracted many invaders. Nadir Shah came and invaded India in 1739 and took away this throne, Takht-I-tawoos, with him. The monuments built by Moghuls show the splendour of their times and gems were very integral to it. Taj Mahal is living example of the use of precious stones in buildings. Jade, cornelion and other gems were used by the Moghuls in plenty.

The Greek writer Thiophratus who lived in 287 BC had written a book on Diamonds and gems. After him Pliny (62-113 AD) wrote in his book on Natural History about gems in detail. In 13th century Marco polo visited India, China, Burma and Ceylon(Sri Lanka), and he wrote about the treasures and jewels in these countries in detail.

Legend and Mythology:

As per the legend associated with the gems, it is said that the king of the demons WALI came to the Indralok-the Heaven. He wanted to win over the Heaven and all the Gods. In Heaven, he was escorted by Indra himself under the guise of a Brahmin seeking to find an animal for propitiation. Indra pleaded with Wali to become animal for the sacrifice as he was not getting anyone. It was getting late and his Yagna would be rendered fruitless. Waii accepted it knowing that his body was invincible. This was known to Indra as well and he did not hurt the body of demon king but hit his head with Vajra. The demon king was shattered in to pieces of gems simply because he was a unique creature himself.

It is said in mythology that from the bones of demon king Wali, Diamonds were found; from his teeth the Pearls; from his blood drops Ruby; from the gall bladder Emerald; from his eyes came out Blue Sapphires; from the juice of his heart came Lapis Lazuli; from his bone marrow appeared Karketan; from his nails appeared Cat's eye; from his body fat came Rock crystal; from flesh came Coral; from skin came out Yellow Sapphire; from his semen appeared gem called Bheesham.

The legend further goes that from these gems, Sun took away Ruby, Moon picked up Pearls, Mars took away Coral, Mercury took Emeralds, Jupiter picked up Yellow Sapphire, Venus took Diamonds, Saturn took Blue Sapphires, Rahu took away Zircon and Ketu lifted Lapis Lazuli. This is the reason why these stones are worn by humans to enhance the strength of these planets.

According to mythology, all these gems had been grown by nature inside the body of demon King Wali as he was a unique creature and when these gems came out of the shattered body, it was symbol of victory of Gods over the demons.

However far-fetched this myth may sound. But one thing is sure that even in ancient times when there was no gemmology or research available, people were aware of wearing gems for strengthening various planets and for propitiation purposes. In all probability, these legends started to grow as people felt the beneficial results after wearing them and in present day we hear a full myth around gemstones.

Beliefs and Gemstones:

Mythology and legends are not convincing to modern generation but some of the communities and cultures still have their beliefs about the usage and effects of various gemstones. About the Amber, it is said that the jewels have been made of the teardrops of a Greek God. According to popular belief in the west, the Amber cures one of rheumatism. In Germany, the garland of Ambers is hung around the neck of the infant, so that their teething takes place without trouble. In Turkey, people believe that by fixing Amber in the Hubble–bubble, the germs would not spread and will be killed even after many have puffed it.

In Greece, people think if wine is poured into the cups made of Amethyst, one does not get drunk after drinking that wine. In Rome, a talisman having Coral pieces is considered very auspicious to quell the bad effects of evil spirits. And Romans used to hang chains made from Coral to the cradle of infants to ward off evil spirits. In ancient China, rings studded with Conch or Oyster shells were believed to cure all aches and ailments of stomach.

In India also, lockets made of silver and studded with Pearls are hung around the necks of the infants to ward off evil spirits. The Greeks still believe, if women wear the Blue Sapphires on person, no sense of immorality would pollute their mind nor any fear of supernatural will affect them.

There are numerous such beliefs cutting across all cultures and communities, which are associated with the gems. These, if written would fill volumes, but a fair idea can be formed from the above that the gems held a very special place in human life since ancient times.

Lordship of Planets Over the Gemstones:

In Vedic astrology, we take into account only nine planets. Seven planets are Sun, Moon, Mars, Mercury, Venus, Jupiter and Saturn and two shadowy planets Rahu and Ketu. These planets have lordship over one stone each as the legend also has described it.

PLANET	GEMSTONE
Sun	Ruby
Moon	Pearl
Mars	Red Coral
Mercury	Emerald
Venus	Diamond
Jupiter	Yellow Sapphire
Saturn	Blue Sapphire
Rahu	Hessonite
Ketu	Cat's eye

These gemstones are used for various conditions of their corresponding planets to derive maximum benefits from them. It is not that only the legend is behind this lordship over the gemstones. We will find out that there is a full scientific reasoning for these lordships and the effect of these gems on human life, if used appropriately.

Science Behind the Effect of Gemstones:

That gemstones work for the betterment of one's life is a known fact. However, many people do not believe in their effects. These days people, especially the younger generation, look for scientific links between the gems and their effects. All astrological reasoning fails to impress them to accept the benefits of the gemstones.

There are laws in pure science which have not been proved but are accepted as their effects are observed by us day in and day out and they are called laws conversely also as they have not been proved otherwise. The simplest example being Law of Gravitation. It is a law because it is observed daily by us and also it has not been proved through experiment to be not true.

Similarly, the effects of the gemstones are observed by those who use them under proper guidance. Since the effects are very subjective and individual in nature, they are not in the scrutiny of public and people at large do not believe in their beneficial values.

The gemstones have different colours and lustre. Sun being the source of all energy, also affects human beings. If we observe the sunlight through prism in a laboratory, we get seven-colour spectrum. The other invisible two colours are infra red and ultra violet. Thus the spectrum of nine colours is understood to be the cosmic matrix and is the very essence of nine planets. The nine planets are associated with these colours and the stones prescribed are also in consonance. It is important to note that the wavelength of coloured light emanating from the nine planets is believed to match those radiating from each planet's corresponding gemstone. Thus, prescribing gemstones is not out of synchronous with this energy system. A particular stone absorbs all kind of solar and cosmic energy and allows a particular type of energy to pass through it and which is then absorbed by the body. If prescribed properly, this actually helps the individual. This restores the balance in him, and he finds the improvement in terms of physical, emotional or in a holistic manner.

Moreover, the effects of gemstones have been proved conversely also. If a person is prescribed a wrong gemstone, it has been observed to adversely affect him as long as he wears it and the effect goes away once the stone is removed. Thus, the efficacy of gemstones do not require laboratory experiments just the way some of the pure science laws do not require experiment in their support.

Among all the elements in nature, **GEMSTONES** constitute the purest, most potent and concentrated forms of colour, and therefore GEMS naturally resonate harmoniously with the energies emanated from their associated planets.

In astrology we are concerned with only seven planets and two shadow planets. The natural frequency of vibration of these seven planets has been calculated and is in agreement with the specific part of the spectrum. In astrology, Rahu is like Saturn and Ketu is like Mars. But these two planets are considered to be karmic as well. Hence, Rahu actually corresponds to Ultraviolet part of spectrum and similarly Ketu corresponds to the Infrared part of the spectrum. This is clear from the sequence of the Electromagnetic spectrum. The Violet to red is the visible part of the spectrum. The Ultra violet and infrared part are not visible, very similar to the nature of Rahu and Ketu. It can be seen that Infrared is after Red which is colour of Mars and Ultraviolet is after Violet which is colour of Saturn.

Spectrum Colour	Corresponding Planet
Ultraviolet	Rahu
Violet, Indigo and Blue	Saturn
Green	Mercury
Yellow	Jupiter
Orange Red	Sun
Red	Mars
Infrared	Ketu

The colour for Venus and Moon actually is white but in case of Venus it is sparkling white while for Moon it is milky white. As we know that combination of all these seven colours of the visible spectrum form white colour.

Thus it can be seen that the stones over which these planets have lordship as discussed earlier, correspond to the colour of the spectrum and hence the corresponding frequency in the spectrum.

Astrological Working of Gemstones:

In astrology the gemstones are prescribed for remedial measures. Sometimes we find that a particular planet in chart is weak and due to this the person is experiencing problems. The corresponding gemstone is then prescribed and we observe that beneficial effects are observed. There are basically two types of gemstones as far as discussion about their working is concerned. Let us discuss how these work

1. Transparent Gemstones:

Majority of the gemstones are transparent. Light can pass through them. They work on the principle that Sun energy and the cosmic invisible part of energy is channelised by these transparent stones. They absorb all the radiations and only allow those frequencies to pass through them, which corresponds to their properties. Thus Blue sapphire will only allow the blue range of frequencies to pass through them. The energy is then energized in a particular manner of a single frequency and then it is further absorbed by the body through nerve endings and the body starts experiencing the beneficial effects of the gemstone. This energy affects the energy field of the body and the resultant will help the body function better. The cosmic energy after getting through the gem also experiences a change as per the frequency of the stone and helps in propitiating the corresponding planet. It is well known that the transparent gemstones are very powerful in their effects due to the fact that they just allow the energy to change towards their natural frequency and absorb the unwanted frequencies.

2. Opaque Gemstones:

The other type of gemstones are opaque. They do not allow energy or light to pass through them. They work on the principle of absorption of energy. All bodies absorb energy and consequently emit energy as well. We can see an angry person getting red. At that moment he emits more energy. These opaque gemstones absorb the energy completely. Then they emit energy as per their properties. This emitted energy is absorbed by the body in the same way through the nerve endings and thus the healing and propitiating effects are experienced. The effects of opaque gemstones are less powerful as compared to transparent gems. This is basically due to the loss of energy, in absorbing energy and then emitting Gem specific energy. Transparent gemstone allows more energy to be transformed as compared to an opaque gemstone.Red coral and Pearl are widely used in astrology and are opaque gemstones.

Chapter 3

Gemstones and Their Semi Precious Substitutes

The gemstones, which have been described for various planets, are the precious stones and are very costly. Another difficulty is that sometimes a stone prescribed is not available. A common man is not able to afford these gemstones. In such cases, a semi precious stone can be worn on prescription, which are normally reasonably priced and are readily available also. Although, the cosmic results of these stones are subdued in nature, but for most cases they work well and in only very few cases the astrologer would insist on precious stone. The astrologers prescribe nine gemstones for nine planets.

We will discuss in detail about these nine gemstones and the semi precious substitutes for them also. The gemstones in astrology are prescribed for twin purposes. One of the purpose is to get the benefits of the planet ruling that gemstone or to ward off the evil effects of that planet in day-to-day life. The second use of gemstones is in Medical astrology. Gemstones have healing powers and their general effects on the medical side will also be discussed in addition to the general astrological effects. It must be borne in mind that these are general effects observed for a gemstone. It depends upon the horoscope and many other complex set of factors that a native has in his/her horoscope, that these general effects of stones get modified and every native experiences somewhat different results for the same gemstone. The chemical composition of the stone and its occurrence and connected details have also been discussed briefly for the benefit of the readers.

RUBY

Ruby is the name given to red gem quality corundum. These can be of varying shades of reds to pink. The best rubies are those, which have mystical deep red colour. In Sanskrit, Ruby is called by the name Manikya. In Urdu and Persian it is called Yakoot.

The finest rubies are found in Burma. Thailand, Afghanistan, Vietnam and Pakistan also produce bright rubies. India, USA, Australia and Norway also produce rubies, which are dark to opaque at times.

The chemical composition of ruby is Aluminium Oxide and the formula is Al_2O_3. The specific gravity is 4.00 and the refractive index is 1.76-1.77. The hardness of ruby is 9 with a crystal structure of Trigonal.

The identification of Ruby is a matter of experience. For an ordinary person access to gemmological investigations is not available. A genuine Ruby if kept on the eye will give a cool feeling continuously while a fake one will become warm after some time. A well cut Ruby will show the same colour at the edges, while an imitation piece will show yellowish edges. Moreover, a Ruby when placed in a milk pot will show the milk as red.

Ruby is the stone for **Sun** and is a precious stone. This gem should be worn in the ritualistic way, which has been used for ages and has been found to energise the stone. The ritual of energising Ruby should be done during the auspicious moments of Ravipushya. But this happens only once in a year. Otherwise, consecration of the gem can be done on Sunday or during the period when there is influence of Pushya constellation

Astrological Effects:

The ruby, also called Manek/Manickam, is said to be the stone that bestows name, fame and recognition, besides of course favours from state and government agencies. It confers on the individual the highest position, if sought. The native is never haunted by any fear of poison. The mental thinking becomes easy going and person starts enjoying sound sleep as well.

Medical Effects:

Ruby increases the heart's strength, body flexibility, vitality, tissue regeneration, mitosis, circulation, and protection from psychic attacks, immunity. This stone decreases inflammation, bleeding, infectious diseases, typhoid, bubonic plague, leukaemia, sickle cell anaemia, schizophrenia, heart attack, diabetes. It restores the balance of nerves, liver, spleen, heart, thymus, spinal column, adrenals, and cholesterol.

Semi Precious Substitute:

The semi precious substitute for Ruby is **Red Garnet.** Astrologically it gives the same effect as given by Ruby but the power of this gem is feeble in that sense. Ruby starts giving its astro effects within days but Garnet takes time to start giving effects.

Red Garnet is called Almandine in gemmology and its composition is Iron Aluminium Silicate with chemical formula as $Fe_3Al_2(SiO_4)_3$. The specific gravity is 3.77; Refractive index 1.86-1.87 and a hardness of 7.5 having a crystal structure of Cubic. This is found in garnet Mica schist and has worldwide occurrence.

Red garnet increases vitality. It decreases anaemia, inflammation, depression, psychosomatic illness, haemorrhaging, inflammation, bleeding, gallstones, kidney stones, and anxiety. It helps in restoring balance of blood circulation, hormones, thyroid, white corpuscles, spinal fluid, pituitary gland, and spleen.

PEARL

Pearls are formed in shellfish- especially oysters and mussels. They are formed as a natural defence against an irritant, such as a piece of grit. Layers of aragonite called nacre are secreted around the irritant and then it gradually builds up to form the pearl. Pearls vary in colour from white, white with a hint of pink, brown and even black. This depends upon the type of water and other ambient factors. In Sanskrit, Pearl is known by several names such as Mukta, Shashiratna etc. In Urdu it is known as Mukharid

Natural pearls have been found in Persian Gulf, Gulf of Mannar in Indian Ocean and Red Sea for very long time. These days in Japan and China pearls are made through culture.

The chemical composition of pearls is Calcium carbonate with conchiolin and water. The specific gravity of pearls is 2.71; Refractive index of 1.53-1.68 and a hardness of 3. The crystal structure is Orthorhombic. The nearest chemical formula for pearls is $Ca\ CO_3$, $C_3H_{18}N_9O_{11}.nH_2O$.

Pearl is the precious stone for **Moon**. Imitation pearls are made of glass and are hollow. They are covered with material made of fish shells. If the real pearl is put in the mouth it tastes of sand granules whereas, the fake one tastes of glass. Another way is to look through a lens . In case of real pearls, two points of nucleus can be found which is not there in case of imitation pearls.

The consecration of pearls is done during the moments of Pushya constellation, Sompushya or during the amritsiddhi yoga on a Monday.

Astrological Effects:

The pearl bestows happiness, loyalty and good health to the wearer. It represents the Moon, which is considered the nurturer of the zodiac. It also gives emotional stability, controls anger, calms the mind and provides domestic happiness. For women, it is supposed to add lustre to the face and regulate the menstrual cycle. All auspicious pearls are believed to ensure heirs, wealth and fame also.

Medical Effects:

. Pearl has cooling and calming effects. It increases healing, vitality, fertility, longevity, digestive power of the body. It is known to decrease the effects of hepatitis, gallstones, bleeding, acidity, irritability, anxiety, malignant cancer, bloating and pain. It helps balance body fluids, female reproductive system, functioning of pancreas, liver and kidneys.

Semi Precious Substitute:

The semi precious substitute for Pearl is **Moon Stone and Opal.** Moonstone is basically Orthoclase with a bluish white sheen and hence the name. It is Potassium Aluminium Silicate with hardness of 6 and specific gravity of 2.57 and Monoclinic crystal structure. These are found in Burma, Sri Lanka, India, Madagascar, Brazil, European Alps and Mexico.

Moonstone gives the astrological effects just like that given by the real Pearl. But then its effects can vary drastically. Pearl has the benefit that it can help natives in warding evils of Moon also. But Moonstone and even Opal is good for the purpose of using it as a strengthening stone for Moon.

Moonstone is a stone used for detoxification and fertility. It is very effective in menstrual problems and restores the normal cycle. It also helps alleviate PMS symptoms. It decreases effects of insanity, dropsy, leucorrhoea, bleeding, thirst, high blood pressure, pulmonary consumption, beestings and insect bites, malaria, yellow fever. It balances intestinal tract, lower spinal column, pancreas, and pituitary glands. The stone is very effective in restoring the various body cycles.

Opal is hardened Silica Gel and contains 5-10 percent water. This is non-crystalline unlike other gems and with use it dries out and can have cracks. The Opal, which shows iridescence, is precious and for Moon white opal is used as substitute. It is Hydrated Silica Gel with hardness of 6, Specific Gravity of 2.10 and Refractive Index of 1.37-1.47 with structure being Amorphous. It is found in cavities in sedimentary rocks and Australia is the main producer of Opals. It is also found in USA, Mexico, Brazil and South Africa.

Opal is having cleansing properties. It improves vision and hearing. It is very good for headaches. It also adjusts and balances the nervous system.

RED CORAL

Coral is made up of the skeletal remains of marine animals called Coral Polyps. These tiny creatures live in colonies, which form branching structures as they grow, eventually resulting in coral reefs and Atolls. Most corals are made of Calcium Carbonate and have red, pink, white and blue colours. But black and golden corals are made of a horn like substance called conchiolin. Out of all Red coral is most precious. In India Red coral is known by many names such as Bhomaratna, Angarak mani, Sinduja etc. In Persian it is called Miranga, Majaan.

Red coral is found in Japan, Mediterranean and African coasts. Black and golden coral is found in West Indies and Australia.

Coral has hardness of 3; specific gravity 2.68; Refractive index 1.49-1.66 and Trigonal crystal structure. The chemical formula is Ca CO_3 (or $C_3H_{48}N_9O_{11}$).

Red coral is the precious stone for **Mars**. The real coral is deep hued like vermilion and is spotless. Unreal corals cannot withstand heat and melt. Moreover, the fake coral when rubbed gives audible sound, which the real one does not. The real coral if scratched on floor and then rubbed with oily fingers, becomes smooth again. The fake remains scratched.

The consecration of Coral should be done when the influence of Pushya constellation is there.

Astrological Effects:

The coral is said to negate the evil effects of the planet Mars. On the positive side Mars is said to be the planet of action. Wearing of a coral helps remove obstacles in marriage and also to overcome marital problems. It helps to develop self-confidence and protect married women from widowhood. It also protects children from the evil eye - "drishti/nazar".

Medical Effects:

The main effect of stone is in tissue regeneration and increase in blood cells. It decreases leukaemia, fever, madness, nightmares, asthma, teething troubles, sterility, constipation, jaundice, obesity, rickets, rabies, menorrhagia, varicose veins, anaemia, haemorrhaging, and arthritis. It helps balancing spleen, mucous membrane, bile, spine, circulation, spinal canal, alimentary canal, and nervous system, Thalamus.

Semi Precious Substitute:

The semi precious substitute for Red coral is **Carnelian.** Carnelian is reddish orange variety of Chalcedony. It has hardness of 7; specific gravity of 2.61; refractive index of 1.53-1.54 and Trigonal structure of crystals. It is basically Silicon Dioxide with formula as SiO_2. Best Carnelian is from India.

Carnelian increases fertility, tissue regeneration, elasticity of blood vessels and assimilation. It is helpful in reducing nosebleed, anorexia, fear, rage, gallstones, kidney stones, pollen allergies, and impotence. One of the main functions carnelian does is to balance sexual energies.

It also balances endocrine system, spleen, pancreas, reproductive organs, liver, kidneys, and gallbladder.

HESSONITE

In Sanskrit, Hessonite is known as Gomedak, Rahuratna. In English it is also called as Cinnamon stone. In Arabic, it is called Hazar Yarnani.

Hessonite is Grossular garnet as per gemology and is found in various colours but they are known to derive their name from their first specimen found. This had orange brown colour and this colour is due to manganese and Iron inclusions. The best Hessonite is found in Sri Lanka in metamorphous rocks or gem gravels. In Madagascar, it is generally called as Cinnamon stone. It is also found in Brazil, Canada and Siberia as well as in Maine (California) & New Hampshire in USA.

The chemical composition of Hessonite is Calcium Aluminium Silicate. The chemical formula is $Ca_3Al_2(SiO_4)_3$ It has hardness of 7.25, Specific Gravity of 3.65, Refractive index of 1.73-1.75 and Cubic crystal structure.

The Hessonite is the precious stone for **Rahu**. The consecration of Hessonite has to be in Ravipushya, Gurupushya or any Pushya influenced time. But the gem has to be energized by chanting Mantras for Rahu for good effects.

Astrological Effects:

The gomeda promotes unity in the family, health, wealth and general happiness. Recognition for work, stability in career and happiness from children is also indicated. It improves stamina and security and assures a healthy, long life. It has also been known to improve vision and ward off the evil eye.

Semi Precious Substitute:

Semi precious substitute of Hessonite is **Zircon and Amber.**

Zircon is chemically Zirconium Silicate with formula of $ZrSiO_4$. This stone is famous for being found in colourless form and their resemblance with diamonds. But it can have colours of yellow, orange, blue, red, brown etc. In astrology, the colour of reddish brown for Zircon is used for Rahu. This stone of gem quality is found as pebbles in alluvial deposits and the best comes from Sri Lanka, Brazil, Thailand, Cambodia, Vietnam, Kampucea, Australia, Burma, Nigeria, Tanzania and France also produce Zircon.

Zircon has hardness of 7.5, specific gravity 4.69, refractive index 1.93-1.98 with a Tetragonal crystal structure.

Amber is the fossilized resin of trees. Most Amber is golden yellow to golden orange, but green, red, violet and black Amber has also been found. The chemical composition is mixture of organic plant resins and mainly the formula is $C_{10}H_{16}O$. It normally occurs as nodules or small irregularly shaped masses. When rubbed, Amber produces a negative electrical charge that attracts dust. The most famous deposits are in the Baltic region, particularly along the coast of Poland and former USSR.

Amber has hardness of 2.5, refractive index of 1.54-1.55, specific gravity of 1.08 and Amorphous crystal structure. Amber with golden orange colour is used a substitute for Hessonite.

Effects:

Amber helps in increasing cell regeneration, strenghthens brain and nervous system. It helps decrease catarrh, ulcers, soreness, hay fever, asthma, convulsions, deafness, insanity, earache, headache, toothache, rheumatism, anxiety, and goitre. It provides balancing influence on liver, kidneys, throat, digestive tract, thyroid, inner ear, brain, central nervous system, teething, intestines and stomach, endocrine system. It is very helpful in joint lubrication and provides fluidity to the muscles, increases elasticity of tendons and removes inflammation of tendons.

YELLOW SAPPHIRE

Yellow sapphire is also known as Oriental Topaz. In Sanskrit it is called Guru ratna, Pushparaag and in Persian as Yakkot. In Urdu as Asphar.

It is basically Corundum and comes in many other colours as well. The chemical composition is Aluminium Oxide with a formula of Al_2O_3. The yellow sapphire is mainly found in Queensland and New south Wales in Australia. Even Sri Lanka, East Africa also produces this type of sapphire. The sapphire has hardness of 9, specific gravity 4.00, refractive index 1.76-1.77 with a Trigonal crystal structure.

Actual yellow sapphire should feel heavy when put on one's palm and should be spotless. It should not have layered surface. After being rubbed with a touchstone, it should shine further. A defective or fake piece will give sand like roughness when touched. It can have blackish bubbles in its body. A fake will give different hues of yellow and whitish. A real sapphire would drown in a liquid whereas other fakes will ultimately come to the surface.

Yellow sapphire is the precious stone for *Jupiter.*

Medical Effects:

This stone drastically helps in memory and learning. It is also an effective stone to decrease the effects of snakebite. It helps balancing stomach, gall bladder, spleen, and liver. It helps tackle weakness, shivering feelings, and catarrh. It is also said to help heal leprosy and skin diseases.

Astrological Effects:

A yellow sapphire is for security, wealth and general prosperity. It helps with academic pursuits, business and trade. The yellow sapphire also brings stability in marriage and happiness from children. It protects the liver, lungs, ears and blood circulation. The yellow sapphire should be the choice of a gem for those who want to gain weight.

Semi Precious Substitute:

The semi precious substitute is *Golden Topaz.*

Golden Topaz is actually golden yellow in colour and is sometimes called as Sherry topaz also. Although topaz occurs in other colours also, but golden yellow is in the category of gems. It is basically Aluminium Fluorohydroxysilicate with a formula of $Al_2(F, OH)_2SiO_4$. It is found in igneous rocks and sometimes in alluvial deposits as pebbles also. It is found in USA, Sri Lanka, Burma, former USSR, Australia, Pakistan, Mexico, Japan and Africa.

Topaz has hardness of 8, specific gravity 3.54, refractive index 1.62-1.63 with a crystal structure of Orthorhombic.

BLUE SAPPHIRE

In Sanskrit, blue sapphire is called as Nelashma, neelratna, Shaniratna, Indraneel etc. In Persian it is called as Yakoot or Kabood.

Blue Sapphire is basicaily Corundum and comes in many other colours as well. But traditionally sapphire is associated with blue colour only. The chemical composition is Aluminium Oxide with a formula of Al_2O_3.

Good quality Blue Sapphire is found in Burma, Sri Lanka and India. The best Indian Sapphire is cornflower blue and is found in Jammu and Kashmir. Montana in USA also produces blue sapphire . Cambodia, Brazil, Kenya, Malawi and Colombia also produce this sapphire. The sapphire has hardness of 9, specific gravity 4.00, refractive index 1.76-1.77 with a Trigonal crystal structure.

Real blue sapphire shines by its own rays and does not borrow light. It is very smooth and the colour has special effect as if emerging out of its core. If placed in a transparent milk pot on a full moon night, it will give the bluish colour to the person holding the pot also. An unreal stone would give a depressed blue colour.

Blue sapphire is the precious stone for **Saturn**. The consecration of Blue sapphire should be done on any Pushya constellation day. Otherwise, it can be worn when there is amritsiddhi yoga time or the day is governed by Shani Pushya. It is advisable to wear it in an alloy called Triloha, but sometimes it is prescribed in Gold as well.

Medical Effects:

The stone is said to be increasing eyesight, longevity, and blood flow to organs. It helps decrease rheumatism, sciatica, neurology, epilepsy, hysteria, tumour, reduces fat, arthritis, nerve pains, mental illness, petrochemical and radiation miasms, excessive bleeding, emotional pain and trauma, haemorrhage. It provides balance to intestinal tract, pancreas, lower spinal column, heart, blood, and adrenals.

Astrological Effects:

The blue sapphire adds wealth, widens the sphere of one's influence on other people particularly if one is dealing with the masses. There is also an increase in social status and prosperity. Saturn controls most diseases in the body; by wearing a blue sapphire, one is assured of a long and healthy life.

Semi Precious Substitute:

The semi precious substitute is ***Turquoise and Lapis lazuli***.

Turquoise is one of the first gemstones mined and varies from sky blue in colour to greenish. It is commonly found in microcrystalline, massive form, usually as encrustations or as nodules. Sky blue turquoise from Iran is the best, but in Tibet a greener variety is found. Mexico and USA also produce greener variety. Chile, Australia and England(Cornwall) also produce. The distinct blue colour is due to presence of copper and traces of Iron.

It has hardness of 6, specific gravity of 2.80, Refractive Index 1.61-1.65 and is chemically Hydrated copper aluminium phosphate. The crystal structure is Triclinic and the formula is $CuAl_6(PO_4)_4(OH)_8.5H_2O$.

Turquoise has amazing property of helping in disorders of female reproductive system. It increases eyesight, tissue regeneration and circulation. Turquoise is very effective in headaches and migraines. It also decreases fever, cataracts, and effects of environmental pollution, anorexia, and stress. It balances circulation, tendons, ligaments, throat, thymus gland, and nerves.

Lapis Lazuli is a Blue rock made up of several different minerals, including Lazurite, Sodalite, hauyne, Calcite and pyrite. The colour of Lapis lazuli varies as per composition but the intense blue variety with minor patches of white calcite and brassy yellow pyrite is the best quality. It is usually found as boulders or within limestones. The best quality lapis lazuli is from Afghanistan. Argentinian stone is also of very high quality. Some different shades of blue are also found in USA and Canada.

It has hardness of 5.5, specific gravity 2.80.refractive index 1.50 with Variable crystal structure. The formula is $(Na, Ca)_8(Al, Si)_{12}O_{24}(SO_4)Cl_2(OH)_2$.

Effects:

Lapis lazuli increases strength, virility, vitality, and oxygenation of blood, mitosis, hearing and immune system. It decreases poison, fever, depression, melancholia, neuralgia, spasms, tonsillitis, and anxiety, Hodgkin's disease. Cancer of the larynx, autism, urinary troubles, tuberculosis, hemorrhoids, jaundice, diabetes, insomnia, neurosis, vertigo and dizziness. It helps in balancing emotions, vocal cords, thyroid, esophagus, bronchial tract, bone marrow, skeletal system and Eustachian tube.

EMERALD

In Sanskrit and ancient texts, Emerald is called as Haridraratna, Marakat, and Somya. In Persian, it is known as Jarmurad.

Emerald is basically Beryl gemmologically with presence of chromium and Vanadium, which makes it green .It can have various colours from colourless, blue, pink and golden yellow depending upon the inclusion. It is Beryllium aluminium silicate and formula is $Be_3Al_2(SiO_3)_6$. It is found in granites, pegmatites and schists as well as alluvial deposits. The finest emerald is from Colombia. Other sources are Austria, India, Australia, Brazil, South Africa, Egypt, Norway, Pakistan and Zimbabwe.

Emerald has hardness of 7.5, specific gravity 2.71, refractive index 1.57-1.58 with a Hexagonal crystal structure.

A -real emerald if seen through Chessus filter(glass made), it will look pink. Whereas, the fake one will remain green. Real emerald if rubbed with turmeric on a stone leaves a red residue.

Green Emerald is precious stone for **Mercury**. Emerald should be worn on a Wednesday. It can be worn in gold or even bronze. The consecration of Emerald is done on a Pushya constellation day.

Astrological Effects:

Communications and movement is represented by the planet Mercury for which the stone is emerald. It is generally worn to improve business, trade and communication skills. It sharpens the intellect and removes speech defects. It controls nervous energy and channelises it in the right direction. Skin problems and allergic conditions are said to improve by wearing an emerald.

Medical Effects:

The general effects of emerald are relating to mind, which means it increases memory, intuition, communication and intelligence. In addition it enhances eyesight, body vitality, and immune system. It is useful in decreasing pain, cancer, asthma, ulcers, infections, childbirth pains, eyestrain, stress, paranoia, schizophrenia, radiation effects, acidity, headache, back pains, sciatica, and female diseases. The effects are achieved as emerald balances the breathing system, nervous system, circulation, nerves, haemoglobin, adrenals, and pancreas.

Semi Precious Substitute:

The semi Precious substitute for this is *Peridot.*

Peridot is the gem quality specimen of the mineral Olivine. Peridot has olive or bottle green colour due to presence of Iron .It is chemically Magnesium Iron Silicate. It is found in St. John's island in Egypt, in China, Burma, Brazil, Hawai and Arizona USA, Australia, South Africa and Norway. The formula of Peridot is $(Mg, Fe)_2SiO_4$.

The hardness of Peridot is 6.5, specific gravity 3.34, refractive index 1.64-1.69 with Orthorhombic crystal structure.

Effects:

Peridot helps body in recuperation and heals fast. It provides body strength and helps tissue regeneration. It is known to decrease anger, jealousy, stress, and epilepsy, poison effects and effects of bites. The stone balances endocrine system and nerves. It aligns and balances inner body, organs, liver, astigmatism, and nearsightedness. It helps in childbirth and is a detoxifier.

CAT'S EYE

In Sanskrit, it is called Vaidoorya, Hemavaidoorya, Vodooraja and Keturatna. In Hindi, it is called Lahsuniya. In Arabic, it is called Enulahara.

Cat's eye is basically Chrysoberyl gemmologically. It occurs in a range of colours from green to yellow to brown. It is a hard and durable stone. This stone when cut en-cabochon, has a near white line across the stone and gives the effect of a cat's eye, hence the name. This effect is due to canal or feather like fluid inclusions, or needle like inclusions of rutile. The highly prized colour for this is light golden brown often with a shadow that gives a light and dark 'Milk and Honey' effect. It is mainly Beryllium aluminium Oxide with a formula $BeAl_2O_4$. The best stone is found in Urals in mica schists.Sri lanka, Burma, Brazil, Zimbabwe, China also produce Cat's eye.

The hardness of this stone is 8.5, specific gravity 3.71, refractive index 1.74-1.75 and Orthorhombic crystal structure.

Cat's eye with yellow tinge in it and whitish ray of eye effect are good quality. The ray should be straight for good quality stone. It is not an expensive stone and should not be bought if cracked, depressed, with a burnt look or dotted. It is said that a Cat's eye when pressed between the two eyes, where third eye of lord Shiva is believed, then the person can see future events.

Cat's eye is the precious stone for **Ketu.** Cat's eye should be worn in Panchdhatu (alloy of five metals). The time for consecration is any moment of Pushya constellation. Except Sundays, it can be worn during Amrityoga.

Effects:

The cat's eye gives a miraculous lift to a sagging career or business and trade. It has the ability to calm the mind, provide patience, and control the wandering thoughts. It is good for attaining enlightenment - moksha, and meditation. It has the power to cure chronic diseases.

Semi Precious Substitute:

The semi precious substitute for this is **Alexandrite.**

Alexandrite is also chrysoberyl with the same composition as cat's eye and the same physical properties described above. The very rare and valuable Alexandrite changes from green in daylight to red, mauve, or brown under incandescent light. It is best when it is transparent and differs only that when cut, it does not produce the effect of a white line across it. Its effects are similar to that of Cat's eye.

DIAMOND

In Sanskrit, Diamond has been named as Heerak, Kulish, Heer, and Abhedya. In Arabic it is called as Alpaas.

Diamond is the hardest mineral on earth, and combined with its exceptional luster and brilliance, is the most prized of all gems. Pure and colourless diamond is the most popular but other varieties like yellow, brown, green, pink, blue and red, even black are also found. Diamond is chemically Carbon and the formula is C. Because of the uniform arrangement of the carbon atoms, diamond crystals are well formed. Diamond forms at very high temperatures and pressures like 80 KM under ground.

These days Australia is main producer. Ghana, Sierra Leone, Zaire, Botswana, Namibia, USA, former USSR and Brazil also produce Diamonds. Diamonds are graded for four "C"s for gem quality—Colour; Clarity; Cut; Carat i.e. weight.

Diamond has hardness of 10.specific gravity 3.52, Refractive index 2.42 with a Cubic crystal structure. A diamond should feel cool when touched especially with tongue. A genuine diamond has unique radiance which glass made fakes do not have.

Diamond is the precious stone for **Venus**. It should be worn in gold or silver only. It can be consecrated on Pushya constellation time.

Effects:

The diamond is said to add a certain charm to the wearer's personality besides bestowing luxuries and comforts too. There is an increase in material wealth, fame and enhancement of artistic abilities. It brings romance and a general zest into one's life. Sexual deficiencies are reduced and disorders are dispelled. It is said that it helps mitigate fever.

Semi Precious Substitute:

The semi precious substitute for this is **Tourmaline and Rock Crystal**.

Tourmaline is basically complex Borosilicate gemmologically. The formula for this is $Na(Li, Al)_3Al_6(Bo_3)Si_6O_{18}(OH)_4$ It comes in various colours and has different names as well, but the colourless tourmaline is called Anchorite and is used for Venus. This variety occurs in pegmatites of Madagascar and Pala(in California in USA).

The hardness of Anchorite is 7.5, specific gravity 3.06, refractive index 1.62-1.64 with Trigonal structure.

Tourmaline helps in sleep disorders and is widely used for this. The stone decreases fear, worry and stress and helps increase sleep. It also acts as a balance force for eyes, brain, thymus and thyroid.

Rock crystal is Quartz and is the most common mineral of the earth. It is Silicon Dioxide with a formula SiO_2. The crystals are usually found as hexagonal prisms with pyramidal ends. It is found worldwide but the most important sources are Brazil, Swiss and French Alps, Madagascar, USA, former USSR.

The hardness of this stone is 7, specific gravity 2.65, refractive index 1.54-1.55 with a Trigonal crystal structure.

Quartz helps increase lactation, tissue regeneration, eyesight, and detoxification. It helps decrease anaemia, jaundice, asthma, constipation, headache, fever, pain, ulcers, leukaemia, bubonic plague, radiation protection, sore throat, gland swellings, vertigo, dizziness, burns and blisters. It balances cell salts, circulation, amino acids, protein, stomach lining, immune system, pituitary gland and intestines.

READY RECKONING TABLE SHOWING
Precious Gemstones and their Semi Precious Substitutes.

Precious Gemstone	Semi Precious Substitute
Ruby	Red Garnet
Pearl	Moon Stone & Opal
Red Coral	Carnelian
Hessonite	Zircon & Amber
Yellow Sapphire	Golden Topaz
Blue Sapphire	Turquoise & Lapis Lazuli
Emerald	Peridot
Cat's Eye	Alexandrite
Diamond	Tourmaline & Rock Crystal

Chapter 4

Other Semi Precious Gemstones

We have discussed nine primary precious gemstones, which are used for astrological purposes as having co-relation with nine planets. In addition, we also have discussed the semi precious substitutes for these nine gemstones, which give the effects of those nine planets. These are cheaper and are easily available. But nature has given us many other abundantly available gemstones of various colours and their effects are also different.

These gemstones are also Semi precious and are used frequently in Jewelry. But even these stones have effects if they are worn in right size and at right time. They also energize the nerve endings of human body thus transferring the cosmic effects in a way typical of the stone's characteristics. These stones also have a ruling planet and give astrological effects. Though these effects are much more mild in comparison to the precious gemstones for the same planet.

Many of these semi precious stones give the effect of more than one planet as well. This makes such stones somewhat unique, though they are abundantly available and cheaper as well.

Many of these gemstones are used in Jewellery and are classified as coloured stones. Generally, the size of these stones used in Jewellery is very small to give any perceptible effect of the connected planet. Moreover, a person does not always wear the Jewellery, hence, the effect if at all there is not persisting enough to give effects of the planet associated with it. But if worn in a prescribed manner and regularly in right size, these stones also give effects of planets associated with them albeit in mild form.

Many of these stones have their unique effects as they give effects of more than one planet combined. These effects also have been discussed. Many stones give effects, which are a result of empirical observation through the ancient times as it is very difficult to classify these stones to a single planet ruler ship. We discuss the most widely used stones in this category.

ADULARIA

Adularia is colourless orthoclase and is alkali feldspar. It is named because of a transparent variety found in Adular Switzerland. Sometimes it exudes a bluish white sheen called adularescence. It occurs in intrusive igneous rocks and is one of the main constituents of granite pegmatites. Best variety occurs in Madagascar and it is also found in Burma and Sri Lanka.

It has hardness of 6, specific gravity 2.56, refractive index 1.51-1.54 and a monoclinic crystal structure. Its composition is Potassium Aluminium Silicate with a formula of $KAlSi_3O_8$. It is a substitute stone for DIAMOND.

AMAZONITE

Amazonite is a form of alkali feldspar and is called microcline. It occurs in many colours but the semi opaque, blue-green variety is of gem quality. The colour is striking and is due to the presence of lead. The most important source is India and it is found in USA, Canada, Madagascar, Tanzania and Namibia.

It has hardness of 6, specific gravity 2.56, refractive index 1.52-1.53 and a triclinic crystal structure. Its composition is Potassium Aluminium Silicate with a formula of $KAlSi_3O_8$. It is a substitute stone for *TURQUOISE.*

Effects:

Amazonite is excellent stone for those who work or live in harsh, toxic, or fast paced environments because of its ability to soothe the nervous system and absorb negativity. It is recommended for people having any type of nervous disorder, such as nervous jitters, sleeping trouble, feelings of being overwhelmed, etc. It also helps overcome criticalness and defensiveness as well as increases the ability to work with others. It can relieve congestion and inflammation in the joints. It helps one to break through their fears. It can also help one with problems of anger, blaming others, or those who are feeling despondent and lonely.

AZURITE

Azurite is an azure-blue copper mineral, occasionally found as prismatic crystals, but more usually in massive form intergrown with Malachite. It is found mainly in copper-mining areas such as Australia, Chile, former USSR, Africa, and China.

It has hardness of 3.5, specific gravity 3.77, refractive index 1.73-1.84 and a monoclinic crystal structure. Its composition is Copper hydroxycarbonate with a formula of $Cu_3(OH)_2(CO_3)_2$. It is a substitute stone for combined influence of **EMERALD** & *BLUE SAPPHIRE.*

Effects:

Azurite helps to balance blood chemistry and is used for prescription in cases where blood disorders are being treated. The treatment should not be stopped, but the stone should be used conjunct. It also helps in clearing sinuses. It is also placed along spine for strengthening the back.

APATITE

Apatite is an abundant mineral found in many types of rock, but gem quality is associated with pegmatites.Blue Burmese Apatite is strongly dichoric and shows colourless or blue when viewed from different angles. The other areas that produce it are Srilanka, Africa, Sweden, Spain and Mexico.

It has hardness of 5, specific gravity 3.20, refractive index 1.63-1.64 and a Hexagonal crystal structure. Its composition is Calcium Phosphate with a formula of $Ca(F, Cl)Ca_4(PO_4)_3$. It is a substitute stone for *BLUE SAPPHIRE.*

Effects:

Apatite is known to help people with stuttering. It helps in clearing the brain to formulate new ideas. It balances thymus, thyroid and tonsils and can be used for diseases arising out of imbalance of these glands.

ANGLESITE

Anglesite is usually colourless with a slight yellow tinge. Its crystals are heavy but fragile and soft. Anglesite is formed by oxidation of galena(lead sulphide) and may be found in Anglesey in Wales and in the lead hills district of Scotland. The best quality is found in Tsumeb(Namibia) and Morocco.

It has hardness of 6.5, specific gravity 6.35, refractive index 1.87-1.89 and an orthorhombic crystal structure. Its composition is Lead sulphate with a formula of $PbSO_4$. It is a substitute stone for *YELLOW SAPPHIRE.*

Effects:

Its effects are similar to the effects of Yellow sapphire. It gives a person ability to advise others and helps in medical conditions as Pleurisy and even asthama.It adds to the wealth of native and protects liver from various diseases.

BERYLLONITE

Beryllonite crystals are colourless, white or pale-yellow, but its weak fire and low dispersion make it a dull gemstone. In addition, it is soft and fragile. It is a pegmatite mineral and is found associated with the mineral sphenakite and berylin in Maine USA. It is also found in Finland and Zimbabwe. It is named after beryllium content in it.

It has hardness of 5.5, specific gravity 2.83, refractive index 1.55-1.56 and a monoclinic crystal structure. Its composition is Sodium Beryllium phosphate with a formula of $NaBePO_4$. It is a substitute stone for *DIAMOND.*

BRONZITE

It is Hypersthene-an iron-rich pyroxene. It is distinguished by its reddish iridescence, which is due to platy inclusions of goethite and hematite. It has colour of greenish brown and bronze like luster. It is mainly found in Austria.

It has hardness of 5.5, specific gravity 3.35, refractive index 1.65-1.67 and an orthorhombic crystal structure. Its composition is Iron Magnesium Silicate with a formula of $(Fe, Mg)SiO_3$. It is a substitute stone for **HESSONITE** and **ZIRCON**.

BLUE TOPAZ

Topaz is found in many colours and many blue topaz varieties are made by heat-treating the colourless topaz. It occurs in igneous rocks such as pegmatites, granites and volcanic lavas. It has also been found in alluvial deposits as water worn pebbles. It is found in Brazil, USA, Sri lanka, Burma, Australia, and Pakistan.

It has hardness of 8, specific gravity 3.54, refractive index 1.62-1.63 and an orthorhombic crystal structure. Its composition is Aluminium fluorohydroxysilicate with a formula of $Al_2(F, OH)_2SiO_4$. It is a substitute stone for **BLUE SAPPHIRE.**

CITRINE

Citrine is yellow or golden yellow variety of quartz. The yellow coloration, due to the presence of iron, is also responsible for the name. Natural citrine is usually a pale yellow. Gem quality citrine is actually rare and is found in Brazil, Spain, and Madagascar.

It has hardness of 7, specific gravity 2.65, refractive index 1.54-1.55 and a Trigonal crystal structure. Its composition is Silicon Dioxide with a formula of SiO_2. It is a substitute stone for **YELLOW SAPPHIRE**.

Effects:

Citrine is a great help in assimilation of vitamins and also helps in tissue regeneration. People with vitaminal debility and atrophy of tissues are prescribed this to help their other treatments. It increases circulation and vision. It helps in appendicitis, gangrene and other degenerative disorders. It has property of balancing thyroid, colon, liver, digestive organs and circulation.

CELESTINE

Celestine is usually found as colourless, milky white prismatic crystals or in fine-grained masses. It is extremely fragile. It may occur with sand stones or limestones, in evaporite deposits, in pegmatites, incavities in volcanic rocks, or with galena and sphelarite in mineral veins. It is found in Namibia or Madagascar.

It has hardness of 3.5, specific gravity 3.98, refractive index 1.62-1.63 and an orthorhombic crystal structure. Its composition is Strontium Sulphate with a formula of $SrSO_4$. It is a substitute stone for **DIAMONDS.**

CALCITE

Calcite is the principal ingredient of limestone and marbles, and most of stalactites and stalagmites. It can also be found as large, transparent, colourless, complex crystals, or as prismatic crystals intergrown with other minerals. Italy is famous for the best variety.

It has hardness of 3, specific gravity 2.71, refractive index 1.48-1.66 and a Trigonal crystal structure. Its composition is Calcium carbonate with a formula of $CaCO_3$. It is a substitute stone for **MOON STONE.**

Effects:

Calcite has yellow colour and works very well mainly with digestive and eliminative organs, such as kidneys, pancreas, and spleen. It tends to detoxify body by absorbing physical disharmony. It helps to balance calcium levels in the body as well as to balance the emotions. It helps the body metabolize mucous and fat and convert it into energy. It helps to purify and balance the blood.

DANBURITE

Danburite is generally colourless but may be yellow or pink as well. The yellow variety is gem quality . They form wedge shaped prisms similar to those found in quartz. Since it was first found in Danbury, Connecticut USA, hence the name. Gem quality is found in Burma, Mexico, Italy, Japan and Switzerland.

It has hardness of 7, specific gravity 3.00, refractive index 1.63-1.64 and an orthorhombic crystal structure. Its composition is Calcium borosilicate with a formula of $CaB_2(SiO_4)_2$. It is a substitute stone for **YELLOW SAPPHIRE**.

DIOPSIDE

Diopside is usually bottle green to light green. The more iron rich and magnesium poor they are, the darker the colour. Very bright green Diopside is coloured by chromium and is called chrome diopside. It is found in USA, Italy, Burma, Siberia, Pakistan, Suth Africa.

It has hardness of 5.5, specific gravity 3.29, refractive index 1.66-1.72 and a monoclinic crystal structure. Its composition is Calcium Magnesium Silicate with a formula of $CaMg(SiO_3)_2$. It is a substitute stone for **EMERALD.**

DUMORTIERITE

Dumortierite is best known in its massive form, which makes an attractive violet and blue decorative stone when polished. It is found intergrown with rock crystals. Most gem quality mineral is found in Nevada USA and is also found in France, Madagascar, Sri Lanka, Canada, Namibia, and Italy.

It has hardness of 7, specific gravity 3.28, refractive index 1.69-1.72 and an orthorhombic crystal structure. Its composition is Aluminium Iron borosilicate with a formula of $Al_7(BO_3)(SiO_4)_3O_3$. It is a substitute stone for **TURQUOISE.**

Effects:

Dumortierite works with veins, arteries, and the whole circulatory system. It is helpful when one is recovering from severe shock or trauma. It gives mental balance. It helps balance water in the body. It helps keep balance in stressful situations and nourishes and strengthens the mind. It helps one to understand strange occurrences better. It can help align the spine.

FIRE AGATE

Fire agate is basically Chalcedony family of microcrystalline quartzes. These are either solid coloured stones, or have bands or moss like or dendritic inclusions. The distinctive iridescent colours of fire agate are caused by layers of iron oxide within the quartz. It is found in Arizona USA and Mexico.

It has hardness of 7, specific gravity 2.61, refractive index 1.53-1.54 and a Trigonal crystal structure. Its composition is Silicon Dioxide with a formula of SiO_2. It is a substitute stone for *CORAL.*

HELIODOR

Heliodoris is a yellow or golden yellow form of beryl and has always been linked with Sun. Gem quality specimens are occasionally found, but more usually inclusions of fine, slender tubes are present, which are visible to the naked eye. It is found associated with aquamarine in granitic pegmatites. The best-quality stones are found in the Urals, Brazil, Madagascar, Ukraine, Namibia and USA.

It has hardness of 7.5, specific gravity 2.80, refractive index 1.57-1.58 and a Hexagonal crystal structure. Its composition is Beryllium Aluminium Silicate with a formula of $Be_3Al_2(SiO_3)_6$. It is a substitute stone for *YELLOW SAPPHIRE.*

IOLITE

Violet blue Iolite is also known as cordierite and has been named as water sapphire due to its similarity with blue sapphire. It is dichoric and gives colourless appearance when viewed across. Gem quality Iolite is found in alluvial deposits as small, transparent, waterworn pebbles in Sri Lanka, Burma, Madagascar and India.

It has hardness of 7, specific gravity 2.63, refractive index 1.53-1.55 and an orthorhombic crystal structure. Its composition is Magnesium Aluminium Silicate with a formula of $Mg_2Al_4Si_5O_{18}$. It is a substitute stone for *BLUE SAPPHIRE.*

Effects:

Iolite helps in decreasing liver function, fatty deposits. It helps in malaria and other fevers as well. It can be helpful in restoring male female hormone balance also.

JADEITE

It is also called jade and is made up of interlocking, granular pyroxene crystals, occure in a wide range of colours. The most prized variety, imperial jade, is a rich emerald green, due to chromium. Jadeite has a dimpled surface when polished. It is found in metamorphic rocks and as alluvial deposits and boulders. The most important source of Jade is Burma and also occurs in Guatemala, Japan and California USA.

It has hardness of 7, specific gravity 3.33, refractive index 1.66-1.68 and a monoclinic crystal structure. Its composition is Sodium Aluminium Silicate with a formula of $Na(Al, Fe)Si_2O_6$. It is a substitute stone for **EMERALD.**

Effects:

Jadeite is balancing. It relaxes heart. It can assist with arthritis by placing it on painful joints. If placed over the eyes it will help with night blindness. It is a general spirit uplifter .It tones up the gall bladder. It is a strong detoxifier and also helps clear sinuses.

KORNERUPINE

Kornerupine was found in gem quality in 1912 and it is not available readily. It is strongly pleochoric, it appears green or reddish brown when viewed from different directions. To show best colour, it is cut with the table facet parallel to the length of the crystal. It is found in Madagascar, Sri Lanka, and East Africa.

It has hardness of 6.5, specific gravity 3.32, refractive index 1.66-1.68 and an orthorhombic crystal structure. Its composition is Magnesium Aluminium borosilicate with a formula of $Mg_4(Al, Fe)_6(Si, B)_4O_{21}(OH)$. It is a substitute stone for **EMERALD.**

MORGANITE

Morganite is beryl and is coloured by manganese impurities and pink, rose, peach and violet are the colours found. It tends to occur as short and stubby prisms, and is dichoric and shows two different tinges of colour, It was found with tourmaline for the first time and the finest variety is from Madagascar. Brazil produces pure Pink crystals and it is also found in Mozambique, Namibia, Zimbabwe and Pakistan

It has hardness of 7.5, specific gravity 2.80, refractive index 1.58-1.59 and a Hexagonal crystal structure. Its composition is Beryllium Aluminium Silicate with a formula of $Be_3Al_2(SiO_3)_6$. It is a substitute stone for *RUBY.*

Effects:

It gives emotional strength and is good for lungs. It promotes relaxation and deep breathing. It heals joints allowing greater flexibility and movement. It helps drain the lymph system. It decreases asthma and tuberculosis. It can be used along with the other treatments.

PHENAKITE

Phenakite is a rare mineral, found as white or colourless tabular crystals or stubby prisms. Twinning is common and distinguishes it from rock crystal. It occurs in pegmatites, granites and mica schists.The best crystals are found in Urals, Brazil, USA, Italy, Sri Lanka, Namibia, and Zimbabwe.

It has hardness of 7.5, specific gravity 2.96, refractive index 1.65-1.67 and a Trigonal crystal structure. Its composition is Beryllium Silicate with a formula of Be_2SiO_4. It is a substitute stone for *DIAMONDS.*

PINK SAPPHIRE

This is basically corundum. It is coloured by very small quantities of chromium and with increasing amount of chromium, it forms a continuous colour range with ruby. Pink sapphires, from a very pale and delicate pink to a near red, occur in Sri Lanka, Burma, and East Africa.

It has hardness of 9, specific gravity 4.00, refractive index 1.76-1.77 and a Trigonal crystal structure. Its composition is Aluminium Oxide with a formula of Al_2O_3. It is a substitute stone for **RUBY**.

PHOSPHOPHYLLITE

This mineral crystals are found prismatic or with a thick tabular habit and range from colourless to deep bluish green. The colourless variety is preferred in astrology. The finest variety is from Bolivia, Germany and USA.

It has hardness of 3.5, specific gravity 3.10, refractive index 1.59-1.62 and a monoclinic crystal structure. Its composition is Hydrated Zinc Phosphate with a formula of $Zn_2(Fe, Mn)(PO_4)_2.4H_2O$. It is a substitute stone for **DIAMONDS.**

ROSE QUARTZ

Pink or peach-coloured quartz is called rose quartz. Its colour is thought to be due to the presence of small amounts of titanium. It is found in massive lumps and in pegmatites. The best material is from Madagascar, but Brazil produces a greater quantity. Other site is Scotland, former USSR, Colorado USA, and Spain.

It has hardness of 7, specific gravity 2.65, refractive index 1.54-1.55 and a Trigonal crystal structure. Its composition is Silicon Dioxide with a formula of SiO_2. It is a substitute stone for **RUBY.**

Effects:

Rose quartz increases circulation, assimilation, and fertility. It helps in reducing leukemia, vertigo, wrinkles and blisters. The main effect is in restoring genital imbalance. It also helps balance kidney, liver, lungs balance. Restores red corpuscles, fertility, cell fluid. Basically helps genitals, skin, lungs and kidneys.

SERPENTINE

The name serpentine refers to a group of predominantly green minerals that occur in masses of tiny intergrown crystals. The two main types used in jewellery are bowenite(translucent green or blue green) and the rare williamsite(translucent, oily green, veined or spotted with inclusions). Bowenite is found in New Zealand, China, Afghanistan, South Africa and the USA.Williamsite occurs in Italy, England, and China.

It has hardness of 5, specific gravity 2.60, refractive index 1.55-1.56 and a monoclinic crystal structure. Its composition is Magnesium Hydroxysilicate with a formula of $Mg_6(OH)_8Si_4O_{10}$. It is a substitute stone for **EMERALD.**

SINHALITE

Sinhalite varies from pale yellowish brown to a dark greenish brown. Crystals have distinct pleochroism, showing pale brown, greenish brown, and dark brown when viewed from different directions. Most gem quality Sinhalite is found as rolled pebbles in the gem gravels of Sri Lanka. It is also found in Brazil, former USSR.

It has hardness of 6.5, specific gravity 3.48, refractive index 1.67-1.71 and an orthorhombic crystal structure. Its composition is Magnesium Aluminium Iron Borate with a formula of $Mg(Al, Fe)BO_4$. It is a substitute stone for **YELLOW SAPPHIRE.**

SCHEELITE

Scheelite is quite soft, has high dispersion and good fire, and varies in colour from a pale yellowish white to brown. It is found in pegmatites and metamorphic rocks. It is found in Brazil, Australia, Italy, Switzerland, Sri Lanka, Finland, France, and England.

It has hardness of 5, specific gravity 6.10, refractive index 1.92-1.93 and a Tetragonal crystal structure. Its composition is Calcium Tungstate with a formula of $CaWO_4$. It is a substitute stone for **YELLOW SAPPHIRE.**

SPODUMENE

Spodumene occurs in a range of colours and the gem variety coloured by manganese is lilac pink and is called kunzite. Strong pleochorism is seen in gems. It is found in Madagascar, Brazil, Burma, USA, Canada, Mexico, and Sweden.

It has hardness of 7, specific gravity 3.18, refractive index 1.66-1.67 and a monoclinic crystal structure. Its composition is Lithium Aluminium Silicate with a formula of $LiAl(SiO_3)_2$. It is a substitute stone for **RUBY.**

SCAPOLITE

It is also called as wernerite. It ranges in colour from pink to purple blue to colourless, but the bluish variety is useful in astrology. Crystals are found as prisms that look like sticks. Scapolite is found as crystals in pegmatites and metamorphic rocks like mica schists and sneiss. Localities are Brazil, Burma, Canada, Kenya, and Madagascar.

It has hardness of 6, specific gravity 2.70, refractive index 1.54-1.58 and a Tetragonal crystal structure. Its composition is Complex Silicate with a formula of $Na_4Al_3Si_9O_{24}Cl-Ca_4Al_6Si_6O_{24}(CO_3, SO_4)$. It is a substitute stone for **BLUE SAPPHIRE.**

SILLIMANITE

Sillimanite is blue to green in colour with distinct pleochorism showing pale yellowishgreen, dark green and Blue from different angles. When crystals occur in long slender prisms in parallel groups, resembling fibres, the material is often called fibrolite. It is found in metamorphic rocks and occasionally in pegmatites. Blue stones are found in Burma and are of use astrologically.

It has hardness of 7.5, specific gravity 3.25, refractive index 1.66-1.68 and an orthorhombic crystal structure. Its composition is Aluminium Silicate with a formula of Al_2SiO_5. It is a substitute stone for **BLUESAPPHIRE.**

SODALITE

Sodalite, whose name reflects its sodium content, is found in all shades of blue, and is a major constituent of the rock lapis lazuli.However, unlike lapis lazuli, sodalite very rarely contains brassy pyrite specks. It may contain white streaks of the mineral calcite. It is usually found as masses in igneous rocks. It is found in Canada, India, Brazil, Namibia and USA.

It has hardness of 5.5, specific gravity 2.27, refractive index 1.48 and a Cubic crystal structure. Its composition is Sodium Aluminium Silicate with a formula of $3NaAlSiO_4NaCl$. It is a substitute stone for **BLUE SAPPHIRE.**

Effects:

Sodalite increases endurance and helps calcium absorption. It decreases stress, nervousness, anger, fears and insomnia. It helps in balancing functioning of glands and lymphs, thyroid. Helps balance digestion also.

UVAROVITE

It is basically of garnet group. The attractive, bright green colour of uvarovite is due to the presence of chromium. The crystals are fragile. It occurs in serpentine rocks. The best crystals are found in Urals. Other sources are Finland, Turkey, and Italy.

It has hardness of 7.5, specific gravity 3.77, refractive index 1.86-1.87 and a Cubic crystal structure. Its composition is Calcium chromium Silicate with a formula of $Ca_3Cr_2(SiO_4)_3$. It is a substitute stone for **EMERALD.**

YELLOW ORTHOCLASE

The yellow variety of orthoclase feldspar is usually faceted as step cut because the stone is fragile. The yellow colour is due to the presence of iron. Orthoclase crystals are columnar or tabular prisms, and are often twinned. The best yellow orthoclase is found in Madagascar in pegmatites.

It has hardness of 6, specific gravity 2.56, refractive index 1.51-1.54 and a monoclinic crystal structure. Its composition is Potassium Aluminium Silicate with a formula of $KAlSi_3O_8$. It is a substitute stone for **YELLOW SAPPHIRE.**

PYROPE

This stone also falls under the garnet category. The blood red colour of pyrope is due to the presence of Iron and Chromium in it. Pyrope is found in volcanic rock and alluvial deposits, and may, alongwith certain other minerals, indicate the presence of diamond bearing rocks. It is found in Arizona USA, South Africa, Argentina, Australia, Brazil, Burma, Scotland, Switzerland and Tanzania. The Swiss and South African Pyropes are lighter red than stones from other places.

It has hardness of 7.25, specific gravity of 3.80, refractive index 1.72-1.76 with a cubic crystal structure. Pyrope is magnesium Aluminium silicate with formula of $Mg_3Al_2(SiO_4)_3$. It is substitute stone for RUBY.

SPESSARTINE

This is also a garnet group of stone. Pure spessartine is bright orange, but an increase in the iron content makes the stone dark orange to red even.Spessartine occurs in granitic pegmatites and alluvial deposits. It is found in Sri lanka, Madagascar, Brazil, Sweden, Australia, Burma and the USA.

It has hardness of 7, specific gravity of 4.16, refractive index 1.79-1.81 with a cubic crystal structure. Chemically it is Manganese Aluminium silicate with formula of $Mn_3Al_2(SiO_4)_3$. This is also used as a substitute of RUBY.

GREEN GROSSULAR

There are two varieties of green grossular:one is found as transparent crystals, the other is massive. Massive green grossular from South Africa is called Transvaal jade, as it comes from Transvaal and resembles jade. The transparent green grossular names tsavorite is used mainly as gem. This is also found in Canada, Sri lanka, Pakistan, Tanzania, and mainly Kenya.

It has hardness of 7, specific gravity of 4.16, refractive index 1.79-1.81 with a cubic crystal structure. Chemically it is Manganese Aluminium silicate with formula of $Mn_3Al_2(SiO_4)_3$. It is generally used as a substitute for EMERALD.

ANDRADITE

This is also from granite group. Garnets having titanium and manganese are grouped as Andradite. The most valuable from then is demantoid with emerald green colour, which is due to presence of chromium. This has typical inclusions of asbestos, which are fine and hair like and are called "horsetails". The yellow variety of andradite is called Topazolite. The best Demantoid is found in Urals in Russia, and is associated with gold bearing sands and metamorphic rocks. It is also found in Zaire, Italy and Kenya.Topazolite crystals are found in the Swiss alps and Italian alps in metamorphic rocks.

It has hardness of 6.5, specific gravity of 3.85, refractive index 1.85-1.89 with a cubic crystal structure. Chemically it is Calcium Iron silicate with formula of $Ca_3Fe_2(SiO_4)_3$.Demantoid is used as substitute for *EMERALD*. Topazolite is used as substitute for *YELLOW SAPPHIRE*.

SPHALERITE

This is also called as blende, and is an ore of Zinc. It is usually very dark brown to black in colour, but, occasionally, transparent yellowish brown or green stones are found that can be faceted. These crystals are found in hydrothermal veins with other minerals, such as galena, quartz, pyrite, and calcite. They are found in Spain and Mexico.

It has hardness of 3.5, specific gravity of 4.09, refractive index 2.36-2.37 with a cubic crystal structure. Chemically it is Zinc Sulphide with formula of (Zn, Fe)S. Sometimes it is used as substitute for HESSONITE.

SPINEL

Spinel is found in a wide range of colours due to presence of various impurities and is transparent to almost opaque. Red Spinel coloured by chromium and iron is the most popular, although for many years it was thought to be a variety of Ruby. Blue Spinel is coloured by iron and less commonly by cobalt. Spinel occurs in granites and metamorphic rocks, and is often found in association with corundum. It is found in Burma, Sri lanka, Madagascar, Afghanistan, Australia, Pakistan Italy, and Turkey.

It has hardness of 8, specific gravity of 3.60, refractive index 1.71-1.73 with a cubic crystal structure. Chemically it is Magnesium Aluminium Oxide with formula of $MgAl_2O_4$. Red Spinel is a substitute for RUBY.

FLUORITE

Fluorite was formerly called fluorspar and is found in wide range of colours ranging from yellow, blue, pink, purple, and green. It is found in Canada, USA, South Africa, Thailand, Peru, Mexico, china, Poland, Hungary, Norway, England, and Germany. The use is very limited as gemstone as it is very soft.

It has hardness of 4, specific gravity of 3.18, refractive index 1.43 with a cubic crystal structure. Chemically it is Calcium Fluoride with formula of CaF_2. It is not assigned one planet rulership.

Effects:

Fluorite of purple colour increases hearing and assimilation. It decreases stress, lung cancer, osteoporosis, aftereffects of anaesthesia, pneumonia, anxiety, sexual frustration, virus attack, arthiritis, colds, flu, infectious cankers, herpes, ulcers, infections, and tumors. It balances liver function and lung functions.

HAUYNE

Hauyne forms part of lapis lazuli and is blue to lilac in colour. Intergrown with other minerals, it is seldom found as individual crystals.

Hauyne is found as small, rounded grains in volcanic rocks. Ancient volcanoes of Germany and Morocco are the best-known sources.

It has hardness of 6, specific gravity of 2.40, refractive index 1.50 mean with a cubic crystal structure. Chemically it is complex Silicate with formula of $(Na, Ca)_{4-8}Al_6Si_6(O, S)_{24}(SO_4Cl)_{1-2}$. It is a substitute stone for **BLUE SAPPHIRE**.

AQUAMARINE

The name means seawater. The preferred colour in 19th century was sea green, but today sky blue and dark blue colours are preferred. It is dichoric appearing colourless and blue from different angles. Gem quality mineral is found as hexagonal crystals, which may be upto 1 metre long. The best quality is found in Brazil, where it occurs in pegmatites and alluvial deposits of gravel. Also found in Urals Russia, Pakistan, India and Nigeria.

It has hardness of 7.5, specific gravity of 2.69, refractive index 1.57-1.58 with a hexagonal crystal structure. Chemically it is Beryllium aluminium silicate with formula of $Be_3Al_2(SiO_3)_6$. It is a substitute stone for **BLUE SAPPHIRE**.

Effects:

Aquamarine is very effective in activating thymus. It helps body decrease fluid retention. It decreases cough, toothache and swollen glands. It provides balance to liver, nerves, thymus, immune system, liver, kidneys, spleen, white corpuscles.

TAAFFEITE

It is named as the first specimen of this mineral was found by count Taaffe in Ireland. It has a pale mauve colour and is a rare mineral. Sometimes it is colourless and even red specimens have also been found. It also occurs in Sri lanka, China, and the former USSR.

It has hardness of 8, specific gravity of 3.61, refractive index 1.72-1.77 with a hexagonal crystal structure. Chemically it is Beryllium magnesium aluminium oxide with formula of $BeMg_3Al_8O_{16}$. It can be used as substitute stone for **RUBY**.

BENITOITE

The crystals of benitoite are blue and are shaped like flattened triangles, and have strong dispersion similar to diamonds. These can be confused with blue sapphire.Dichorism is strong in it and it appears colourless from different angles. It occurs in veins in blue schists. The sole source is in San Benito county in California USA, after which the stone is named.

It has hardness of 6.5, specific gravity of 3.67, refractive index 1.76-1.80 with a hexagonal crystal structure. Chemically it is Barium titanium silicate with formula of $BaTiSi_3O_9$.It is a substitute stone for **BLUE SAPPHIRE.**

AMETHYST

Crystalline quartz in shades of purple, lilac, or mauve is called Amethyst. This is a stone, which traditionally is worn to guard against drunkenness, and to instill a sober and serious mind. Amethyst is dichoric, showing a bluish or reddish purple tinge when viewed from different angles. Amethyst is found in alluvial deposits or in geodes and largest deodes are found in Brazil. Amethyst from Urals has reddish tinge, Canadian amethyst is violet. It is also found in Sri lanka, India, Uruguay, Madagascar, Namibia, and Zambia.

It has hardness of 7, specific gravity of 2.65, refractive index 1.54-1.55 with a Trigonal crystal structure. Chemically it is Silicon dioxide with formula of SiO_2.

Effects:

Amethyst increases calm sleep, circulation, red corpuscles. Increases immune system functioning, circulation in legs and feet, tissue regeneration, vision, memory, co-ordination. It decreases stress, tension, insomnia, pain, anger, alcoholism, pimples, rough skin, headaches, kleptomania, depression, drug addiction, colour blindness, autism, dyslexia, epilepsy, diabetes, hypoglycemia, stomachaches, and allergies It balances emotions, sleep, pancreas, pituitary, thymus, thyroid, endocrine system, breathing.

MILKY QUARTZ

This form of quartz derives its distinctive white or cream colour from inclusions of gas and liquid bubbles. The degree of milkiness depends upon the number and size of inclusions present. The crystals are hexagonal prisms with pyramidal ends. Very large crystals are found in Siberia. It is also found in Brazil, Madagascar, USA, and Namibia.

It has hardness of 7, specific gravity of 2.65, refractive index 1.54-1.55 with a Trigonal crystal structure. Chemically it is Silicon dioxide with formula of SiO_2. It is substitute stone for *OPAL*.

Effects:

Milky quartz improves hearing, reduces back pain. It supports deeper breathing. It reduces anxiety by relaxing the chest and promoting deep breathing. It balances blood pressure. It clears stagnation in sinus conditions.

AGATE

Agate occurs in nodular masses in rocks such as volcanic lavas. When split open, they reveal an amazing variety of colours and patterns, and a distinct banding that distinguishes agate from other kinds of chalcedony. Band colours are determined by different impurities present. Moss agate is translucent and colourless, white or grey, with dark, moss like inclusions. The most famous area for agates is Idar-Oberstein in Germany. Moss agate occurs in India, China and USA.

It has hardness of 7, specific gravity of 2.61, refractive index 1.53-1.54 with a Trigonal crystal structure. Chemically it is Silicon dioxide with formula of SiO_2. No specific planet rulership is assigned to it.

CHRYSOPRASE

Chrysoprase is a translucent, apple green colour stone. It belongs to chalcedony group of minerals and was used both by Greeks and Romans as a decorative stone. The colour is due to the presence of nickel, which can fade in sunlight giving it jade like appearance. The best quality mineral these days comes from Queens land Australia, Urals,

Brazil and Austria.

It has hardness of 7, specific gravity of 2.61, refractive index 1.53-1.54 with a Trigonal crystal structure. Chemically it is Silicon dioxide with formula of SiO_2.It can be used as a substitute stone for *EMERALD.*

Effects:

It strengthens eyes. Increases healing process in body and decreases gout, nightmares and depression.

RUBELLITE

Rubellite belongs to tourmaline group of minerals.Rubellite is the name given to the red variety and looks like ruby. Russian pink or red tourmaline occurs in weathered granites. Other places are Madagascar, USA, Brazil, Burma, and East Africa.

It has hardness of 7.5, specific gravity of 3.06, refractive index 1.62-1.64 with a Trigonal crystal structure. Chemically it is complex borosilicate with formula of $Na(Li, Al)_3Al_6(BO_3)_3Si_6O_{18}(OH)_4$.It can be used as a substitute stone for *RUBY.*

Effects:

Rubellite increases fertility and boosts immune system. It decreases gonorrhea and syphilitic miasm, tension, and female cramps. It helps balance body energy, align and heal spine, digestion, heart, lungs, pancreas, reproductive system.

INDICOLITE

Dark blue tourmaline is called indicolite or, occasionally, indigolite.Indicolite is often heat treated to lighten its colour to make it more attractive stone. An important source for indicolite is Siberia, where it occurs in yellow clays formed from weathered granites. Fine, bright blue tourmaline has recently been found in Paraiba, Brazil. It is also found in Madagascar and USA.

It has hardness of 7.5, specific gravity of 3.06, refractive index 1.62-1.64 with a Trigonal crystal structure. Chemically it is complex borosilicate with formula of $Na(Li, Al)_3Al_6(BO_3)_3Si_6O_{18}(OH)_4$.It can be used as a substitute stone for **BLUE SAPPHIRE.**

Effects:

Indicolite increases sleep. It decreases fear, worry, stress. It helps balance lung functions, thymus, thyroid and throat.

ANDALUSITE

Andalusite varies in colour from a pale yellowish brown to a dark bottle green, dark brown, or popular greenish red. It has strong pleochorism. Andalusite is usually found in pegmatites.Pebbles occur in gem gravels of Sri lanka and Brazil. Other places are Spain, Canada, Russia, Australia, and USA.

It has hardness of 7.5, specific gravity of 3.16, refractive index 1.63-1.64 with an Orthorhombic crystal structure. Chemically it is Aluminium Silicate with formula of Al_2SiO_5.It can be used as a substitute stone for **HESSONITE.**

ENSTATITE

Enstatite is one of the pyroxene family which is a series of magnesium to iron rich silicates. Crystals occur as short prisms. It varies in colour from gray to yellowish green or olive green, to an iron rich brownish green. A brilliant emerald green variety coloured by chromium also occurs.Enstatite is often found with kimberlitic in South Africa, Brownish green is found in Burma, Norway and California. It also occurs in USA, Switzerland, Greenland, Scotland.

It has hardness of 5.5, specific gravity of 3.27, refractive index 1.66-1.67 with an Orthorhombic crystal structure. Chemically it is Magnesium Iron Silicate with formula of $Mg_2Si_2O_6$.It can be used as a substitute stone for **EMERALD.**

SILLIMANITE

Sillimanite is blue to green, with distinct pleochorism showing pale yellowish green, dark green, and blue from different angles.Sillimanite is found in metamorphic rocks and occasionally in pegmatites. Blue and violet stones are found in Burma, greenish gray stones in Sri Lanka. Other sites are Czechoslovakia, India, Italy, Germany, and Brazil.

It has hardness of 7.5, specific gravity of 3.25, refractive index 1.66-1.68 with an Orthorhombic crystal structure. Chemically it is Aluminium Silicate with formula of Al_2SiO_5.It can be used as a substitute stone for combined effects of **EMERALD AND BLUE SAPPHIRE.**

TANZANITE

Ziosite occurs in a number of varieties, the most gem quality being Tanzanite, which is blue, coloured due to presence of Vanadium. It has distinct pleochorism, showing either purple blue, or slate gray depending upon angle they are viewed from. Tanzanite was first found in Tanzania, hence the name.

It has hardness of 6.5, specific gravity of 3.35, refractive index 1.69-1.70 with an Orthorhombic crystal structure. Chemically it is Calcium aluminium hydroxy Silicate with formula of $Ca_2(Al, OH)Al_2(SiO_4)_3$.It is a substitute stone for **BLUE SAPPHIRE.**

Effects:

Tanzanite balances potassium levels and strengthens the heart and acts as very effective mood lifter. It helps in balance spine, shins. Very effective in heart conditions and kidney conditions.

BRAZILIANITE

Brazilianite is an unusual gemstone. Its yellow or yellowish green colour is striking. The main locality where it is found is Brazil, where crystals upto 6 inches have been found. Smaller crystals have been mined in New Hampshire in USA.

It has hardness of 5.5, specific gravity of 2.99, refractive index 1.60-1.62 with a monoclinic crystal structure. Chemically it is Aluminium sodium hydroxyphosphate with formula of $Al_3Na(PO_4)_2(OH)_4$. It is a substitute stone for **YELLOW SAPPHIRE.**

MALACHITE

Malachite is often found in green opaque masses, the colour is due to copper content. The crystals are too small for faceting and it is polished to show bands of light and dark green. It occurs in small quantities worldwide, but in large quantities in copper mining areas. Zaire is the most important producer.

It has hardness of 4, specific gravity of 3.80, refractive index 1.85 mean with a Monoclinic crystal structure. Chemically it is Copper hydroxycarbonate with formula of $Cu_2(OH)_2CO_3$.It is a substitute stone for **EMERALD.**

Effects:

Malachite increases fertility, tissue regeneration, blood circulation, immune system and also acts as mood amplifier. It decreases depression, anxiety, stress, hernia, cramps, cardiac pain, cancerous tumours, cholera, colic infection, leukemia, rheumatism, vertigo, ulcers, nervous tension, autism, dyslexia, epilepsy, kidney stones, asthma, arthritis, swollen joints, tumours, broken bones, torn muscles. It helps in balancing pancreas, spleen, lactation, pineal gland, circulation, body fluids, red corpuscles.

Chapter 5

Prescribing Gemstones

The discussion about astrological use of gemstones can not be complete unless the techniques of prescribing gemstones are elaborated. There are basically four methods of prescribing the gemstones. There are various viewpoints regarding prescription of gemstones. Many feel that the gemstones should be worn to negate the ill effect of a planet. Some feel that the gemstone should be prescribed for the Dasa lord, which is operating at the time. Many astrologers prescribe gemstones for strong planets in the chart as well. We will discuss the various methods of prescription here and have also discussed the most scientific way of prescribing the Gemstones which will yield the best effects.

Prescription on the basis of `*Janma Rashi*' or the `*Moon sign*'

In this system of prescription the gemstone is prescribed on the basis of the zodiacal sign in which Moon was posited at the time of birth. The placement of Moon is very significant in Vedic Astrology. Actually, the Vedic system is Moon based and hence this method gives good results. This system can lead to prescription of appropriate stone many times. Wearers, who have worn stones prescribed this way, have many times received adverse results. The basic flaw in the system is that it does not take care of the position of other planets in the horoscope and also loses sight of many other astrological factors. The Moon in a birth chart can go into an adverse house. In such case, Moon sign lord may not be the best benchmark for prescribing the gemstone. The table A shown gives the results of the first method. The Indian names for the planets and the stones have also been given for convenience of the readers.

We will discuss the case of a native who was prescribed gemstone on the basis of Moon sign alone. The chart (Chart-A)shown below is of a senior IAS officer (details withheld). He was prescribed Emerald on the basis of Moon sign being Gemini. He started getting a lot of opposition to his ideas and views both professionally and at home also. He asked the author to look at his horoscope. He was asked to remove Emerald immediately. In this chart, Mercury is the lord of 3rd and 6th houses and does not work like a benefic. The adverse effects of 6th house found manifestation for him i.e. opposition to his views from all sides but being 3rd lord in ascendant, Mercury gave him enough will power as well to withstand it. But later when he removed Emerald, he felt that things improved.

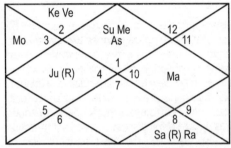

Chart of an IAS Officer - Chart-A

Another case is of a lady who is the wife of an IAS officer. The lady works herself in a private company. The lady was prescribed Emerald as her chart below(Chart-B) shows Moon in Gemini and also in ascendant.

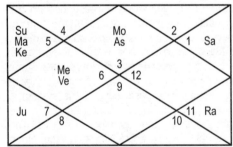

Chart of a Lady - Wife of an IAS Officer (Chart-B)

Here, Mercury is Lagna lord as well as Moon sign lord. Mercury is benefic for her and Emerald has helped her immensely as far as her family life and career advancement is concerned. Readers would appreciate that Mercury is in 4th house and aspects 10th house of profession.

Thus, we can see that gemstones prescribed blindly by using this technique can backfire and also if this technique is used after proper evaluation can help a person.

Prescription on the basis of '*Lagna*' – the '*Birth Ascendant*'

In this system, the gemstone is prescribed on the basis of the sign, which is rising at the time of the birth. The system has a flaw that it does not give credence to any other astrological factor. The stones prescribed this way may not give any effect at times and may adversely affect the native. This can happen when the Ascendant lord owns an adverse house or is placed in an adverse position in birth chart. The Table-A shown below gives a summary of this system of prescription.

TABLE-A

Ascendant/ Moon Sign	Ruling Planet	Gemstone
Aries (Mesha)	Mars (Mangal)	Red Coral (Moonga)
Taurus (Vrish)	Venus (Shukra)	Diamond (Heera)
Gemini (Mithun)	Mercury (Budh)	Emerald (Panna)
Cancer (Karka)	Moon (Chandra)	Pearl (Moti)
Leo (Singha)	Sun (Surya)	Ruby (Manik)
Virgo (Kanya)	Mercury (Budh)	Emerald (Panna)
Libra (Tula)	Venus (Shukra)	Diamond (Heera)
Scorpio (Vrischik)	Mars (Mangal)	Red Coral (Moonga)

Ascendant/ Moon Sign	Ruling Planet	Gemstone
Saggitarius (Dhanu)	Jupiter (Brihaspati)	Yellow Sapphire(pukhraj)
Capricorn (Makar)	Saturn (Shani)	Blue Sapphire(neelam)
Aquarius (Kumbh)	Saturn (Shani)	Blue Sapphire(neelam)
Pisces (Meen)	Jupiter (Brihaspati)	Yellow Sapphire(pukhraj)

This technique can be elaborated by using another chart. The chart below (Chart-C) belongs to a lady. She is the daughter of a senior Police Officer. She was prescribed Blue Sapphire by an astrologer on the premise that it is her birth stone as Saturn is lord of the ascendant i.e. Lagna Lord. Immediately after wearing it, she had to move away from her parents due to her job assignment and felt unhappy.

She contacted the author through a colleague. She was under lot of stress and had even developed back pain, homesickness within a month of wearing the stone. Readers will appreciate that Saturn here is Lagna lord but is debilitated in 4th house. Moreover, Saturn being 2nd lord is having marak propensities as well. This is the reason she had to go away from her family as Saturn is in 4th house debilitated and felt homesick. 4th House being of family. Another aspect in her chart is that she moved to another place with a jump in her salary, which also is due to Saturn being 2nd lord of wealth. Saturn being Marak gave her back pain and laziness as it can not kill the native being lagna lord also.

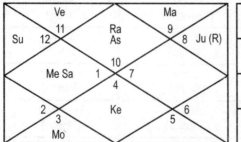

Chart of a lady (Chart-C)

She was asked to remove Blue Sapphire. After around 20 days of removing it, she was recalled to her original place of work as the work had suffered there. She was advised to wear a Diamond for life.

This case shows that the gemstones prescribed considering only ascendant lord in mind and ignoring other astrological rules, can give bad results. Such blind prescriptions should be avoided.

Prescription on the basis of '*Janma Nakshatra*'- the '*Birth Constellation*'

In this system the prescription is based on the constellation (Nakshatra) at the time of birth. The Janma Nakshatra is the Nakshatra where Moon is placed at the time of birth of a native. Vedic Astrology and its dasa system originate out of this nakshatra placement of Moon. Hence, this nakshatra lord commands great influence in the life of native. This system in practice has been used for prescribing gemstones with amazing accuracy. But at times it does not give desired results as this system also ignores other astrological factors during the process of prescription of stones to a native. The table below is ready reckoner form of this system of prescription where based on Janma Nakshatra we can find out the corresponding lordship and the gemstone.

Nakshatra	Ruling Planet	Gemstone
Aswini	Ketu	Cat's Eye
Bharani	Venus	Diamond
Krittika	Sun	Ruby
Rohini	Moon	Pearl
Mrigshira	Mars	Red Coral
Adra	Rahu	Hessonite
Punarvasu	Jupiter	Yellow Sapphire
Pushyami	Saturn	Blue Sapphire
Ashlesha	Mercury	Emerald
Magha	Ketu	Cat's Eye
Poorva Phalguni	Venus	Diamond

Nakshatra	Ruling Planet	Gemstone
Uttra Phalguni	Sun	Ruby
Hasta	Moon	Pearl
Chitra	Mars	Red Coral
Swati	Rahu	Hessonite
Vishaka	Jupiter	Yellow Sapphire
Anuradha	Saturn	Blue Sapphire
Jyeshta	Mercury	Emerald
Moola	Ketu	Cat's Eye
Poorvashada	Venus	Diamond
Uttarashada	Sun	Ruby
Sravana	Moon	Pearl
Dhanishta	Mars	Red Coral
Poorv Bhadrapad	Jupiter	Yellow Sapphire
Uttra Bhadrapad	Saturn	Blue Sapphire
Revathi	Mercury	Emerald

To elaborate this technique, we will discuss another horoscope (Chart-D). This is the chart of yet another IAS officer. Here the ascendant is Cancer and the yoga karaka planet Mars is debilitated in ascendant. His Moon is placed in Mrigsira nakshatra. This Janma Nakshatra for him is Mrigsira and its lord is also Mars. Being a senior colleague of the author, he asked about his health one day.

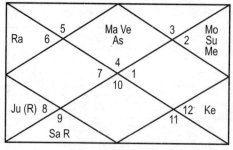

Chart of an IAS officer (Chart-D)

It was pointed out to him that he may be having problems with his blood pressure. He replied in affirmative and told that he is taking some medication as well. Since his blood pressure was found fluctuating even after medication, he asked author some remedy. He was prescribed Red Coral. Mars being his nakshatra lord was debilitated and hence caused him this condition. Mars is otherwise a yoga karaka planet for him and hence Red Coral is well suited for him.

Within a period of 2 months, he found things stabilizing and alongwith prescribed regular puja he found that his blood pressure has been well managed. He has quit medicine after consulting doctor and is doing fine for the last 3 months although he has been advised to keep monitoring.

This case shows that Nakshatra lord, if it does not own evil houses, can be a solid benchmark for prescribing gemstone. Though, the ultimate benefits will depend upon where it is posited as it will then affect that area much more. Here it helped him remarkably in his health as Mars is posited in Lagna itself.

Prescription on the basis of Operating Dasa:

This is a technique in which the gemstones are prescribed as per the Dasa operating in the case of the native. Every birth chart is analysed individually and the effect of the Dasa and antardasa lord are evaluated. The strength of the dasa lord in the chart and varga charts is also assessed. The houses owned by Dasa lord and other connected factors are also assessed deeply. After weighing all these, the appropriate gemstone is prescribed.

This system requires constant monitoring and the gemstone prescriptions are very dynamic here as sometimes the antardasa lord is kept in view while prescribing the stone. Since antardasa changes frequently, dynamic nature of prescription has to be there. Gemstones may require change when the antardasa changes. Due to this dynamism inherent in the system, this can become a costly affair as well.

Another flaw with this method is that the gemstones prescribed on the basis of Dasa will give good and bad effects both. Good effects on an area of life will be observed but the bad effects on some other area will also be there. This system can give wrong results in some cases when the strength of the dasa lord is not evaluated properly. In case the dasa lord owns a bad house, then during its period effects of ownership of a bad house also manifest. A gemstone prescribed for native on the basis of dasa lord will enhance the bad effects as well. Thus, house ownership of dasa lord or antardasa lord becomes a key issue to be considered if the gemstone is being prescribed on the basis of Dasa/antardasa.

In one case, where such prescription gave bad results, is discussed here. The chart below (Chart-E) is that of an IAS officer in whose case Cancer is rising. He was having financial problems and funds were not accumulating rather he was eating into his savings also. When he approached, he was running Rahu/Sun and he had been prescribed the Gemstone Ruby. He explained that it was due to the premise that Sun being antardasa lord and lord of 2nd house, it would benefit his funds position. He did get some opportunities of making money but nothing sustainable was there. Rather, he started suffering from back pain and was bedridden now and then.

He was advised to remove Ruby immediately. The reason being Sun is lord of 2nd house becomes Marak. It is in 8th house and will give health troubles. Thus he was getting these medical problems. After removing the Ruby, he could get his health normal. He was not getting health problems even in Sun antardasa, as Jupiter was aspecting Sun in Transit. But wearing Ruby started the effects and Sun's malefic results started manifesting. Progressively his fund position has improved and his health is also normal now. He was advised to wear Hessonite, which he is wearing.

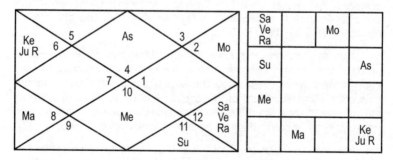

Chart of an IAS officer (Chart-E)

Prescription on the basis of First letter of the *Name*

In this system, the gemstones are prescribed on the basis of the first letter of the name of the person as per Indian sound of pronunciation of that letter. The system gives very indifferent results and is not very popular. The reason is that, in modern times the names are not given on the basis of the astrological consultations by people and the prescription of a gemstone may not be in tune with the actual horoscope of the native. The table below gives the bird's eye view of details of the system.

First Letter of Name	Lord of the Sign and the Sign	Recommended Gem
Choo, chey, cho, laa, lee, loo, leylow, aa	Mars Aries	Red Coral
Ee, oo, ey, o, vaa, vee, voo, vey, vo	Venus Taurus	Diamond
Kaa, kee, koo, ghau, ddau, chhau, ke, ko, haa	Mercury Gemini	Emerald
Hee, hoo, hey, ho, ddaa, ddee, ddoo, ddey, ddo, aa	Moon Cancer	Pearl
Maa, mee, moo, mey, mo, ttaa, ttee, ttoo, ttey	Sun Leo	Ruby
Tto, paa, pee, po, poo, pey, shshau, nnhau, tthau	Mercury Virgo	Emerald
Raa, ree, roo, rey, ro, thaa, thee, thoo, tey	Venus Libra	Diamond
Tho, naa, nee, noo, ney, no, yaa, yee	Mars Scorpio	Red Coral
Yey, yo, bhaa, bhee, bhoo, dhau, phaa, ddaa, bhey	Jupiter Sagittarius	Yellow Sapphire
Bho, jaa, jee, khee, khoo, khey, kho, gaa, gee	Saturn Capricorn	Blue Sapphire
Goo, gey, go, saa, see, loo, ley, low, aa	Saturn Aquarius	Blue Sapphire
Dhee, dhoo, thaw, jhaw, bhaw, dhey.chaa, chee	Jupiter Pisces	Yellow Sapphire

Prescription by a qualified Astrologer - RECOMMENDED

The most specific method is based on the prescription by a qualified Astrologer. The system takes into account various astrological factors before prescribing the gemstone. This is recommended system as it leaves almost nothing to chance and tries to factor in all aspects before prescription. The steps involved in this system are discussed below, but it should be kept in mind that a qualified Astrologer is a prerequisite to make use of this system.

Step 1. — The Lagna is looked at first and then the lord of ascendant is checked for its auspiciousness in the Rasi and Navamsa chart.

Step 2. — Then the position of the planet ruling the Mahadasa (Major Planetary Period) is checked. Sometimes the ruling planet of antardasa is also factored in.

Step3. — Then the Moon Rasi is checked and the lord of Moon sign is checked for auspiciousness.

Step 4. — Then the Janma Nakshatra is checked including the lord and its dispositor for auspiciousness.

Step5. — Next all the nine planets are examined in Rasi chart to see their strengths.

Step 6. — Then the sign ownership of various planets is also given due consideration.

Step 7. — The Navamsa chart has to be studied for all the factors simultaneously as it will pinpoint many hidden facts, which are overlooked by looking at the Rasi Chart.

Step 8. — Then the chalit chart should also be made to see if a planet changes its position housewise. If it does, then it should be invariably taken into account.

The above system will give clear indications about the type of gemstone to be prescribed for a native. Normally the stones are prescribed for strengthening the planets, which results in beneficial effects. The natives, who remain in touch with their astrologers as a counselor, derive more benefits. In such cases, the astrologer is able to prescribe gemstones for a particular period only to derive the maximum benefits of it. Then that gemstone is not used and another gemstone is prescribed for further period. This dynamic way of prescription is actually very beneficial and is gaining ground in modern times.

In order to illustrate this technique, let us discuss some more examples where such analysis was done while prescribing gemstones.

The chart below (Chart-1) belongs to a lady who works in a top multinational company as a human resource executive. The chart shows the presence of a powerful Gaj Kesari Yoga in the chart and Jupiter is vargottam in Navamsa as well (not shown). Yoga karaka Mars is in 9th house of its own. The lady wanted to change her job in the year 2003 when she asked the author about her future. She was not getting any right break and had started to feel a little despondent also. Her Jupiter period was to start in March 2003 and it was told to her that, she would land up a job beyond her expectations involving traveling and of a much higher status as it was predicted that Gaj Kesari Yoga would start giving results. She was asked to wear a Yellow Sapphire immediately. Exactly on 1st April 2003, she joined this new Job in a multinational company with a higher status and huge jump in her salary (around 3 times her present). Thus prescribing a stone after thorough analysis helps in removing impediments and strengthens the presence of good yogas, which were visible in her case anyway.

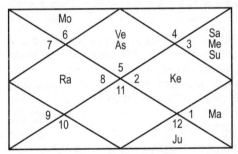

Chart - 1

The chart (chart-2) belongs to an IRS (Income Tax) officer. He was feeling left out in his department though he was holding very key post in his department. He met the author and asked generally about his life and career and asked if he could wear some stone to improve his position. The chart shows that Saturn is debilitated and gets Neechbhanga Rajyoga also. Saturn is Neech Vargottam in Navamsa chart also. Thus, Saturn can be very fruitful planet for him. He was running Dasa of Saturn and antardasa of Rahu. Rahu being in 3rd house has 2:12 relation with Dasa lord Saturn. Saturn is maintaining his Rajyoga effects but Rahu created some stagnation and anxiety for him in career. He was advised to wear Blue Sapphire and was also advised regular Puja. Within a month he has been able to handle his key position very well and has been able to get some cases solved immediately within one month of wearing it but of course with lot of hard work on his part.

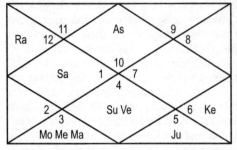

Chart - 2

Another chart (chart-3) belongs to a lady born in London. She landed a very lucrative contract in USA when her Jupiter Dasa started and made around 0.5 million dollars in that contract of 2 years. She met author in Nov 2004, when she was running Jupiter dasa and Mercury antardasa. She wanted to know about her career and wanted some prescription of gemstone for her career.

Jupiter forms a very powerful Gaj Kesari yoga in her chart and is in its own house in birth chart. Mercury is lord of 9th house and 6th house and is placed in 11th house. Mercury is in 8th house in her Dasamsa chart. This shows that the euphoria of Gaj Kesari Yoga would have settled by then to a normal level. She confirmed it to be right. She was asked to wear a diamond for life to have constant support in her career being yoga karaka planet for her and placed in 9th house.

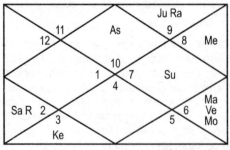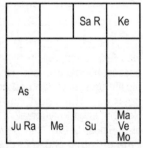

Chart - 3

Another chart (Chart-4) belongs to an Indian Forest Service officer. He worked with the author. He wanted to know about his pursuit of academic activity and also wanted which stone should he wear. He was running Saturn dasa and Venus antardasa. Saturn is in 6th house, which gives him an edge over his rivals and is 7th and 8th lord. Venus is afflicted but is placed strongly in the chart. The lord of his 10th house is exalted and it is lord of 5th house as well. He was asked to wear Red coral, as it is the most potent planet for Cancer Lagna. It would give boost to 5th house affairs of academic activity. After wearing this, he got himself enrolled for PhD in the pratyantar dasa of Mars.

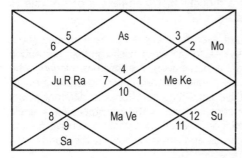

Chart - 4

Another chart is of yet another IAS officer having marital problems. He is a divorcee and is planning to marry again. He wanted to know the suitable gemstone for him. His chart has Lagna lord in 6th house. Moon and Venus aspect each other, which show that he will marry a person chosen by him, which he did, and that marriage failed. Venus as lord of 6th and 11th house is placed in 7th house and is not a good influence in this chart. Mars afflicts 7th house of Navamsa chart as well. Saturn Mars oppose in the birth chart. He has been advised to wear an Emerald to help boost his 7th house lord and also to help him tide over the ill effects of Kendradhipati dosha to Mercury. There have been developments towards his remarriage but the actual marriage has not happened and may fructify in the near future.

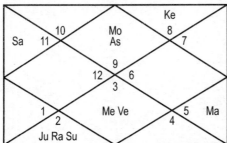

Chart - 5

Conflicting Gemstones:

In modern times it is very important to look for the conflict between various varieties of gemstones. This is more important as these days jewellery has become a highly consumerist business and most of the times the jewelers are not aware of the occult and cosmic power of the gems. This type of jewellery is basically sold for cosmetic and vanity purposes without giving it a thought that they have a cosmic role to play in the lives of humans.

Thus, it is very important even for a layman to have an idea about the conflict of various gemstones so that he himself can take precaution when it is not possible to get expert advice. For those astrologers, who are qualified and prescribe gems, it is equally important area of knowledge. They can prescribe conflicting gemstones at different points of time to derive maximum benefits from all the gemstones for a single native. This dynamic prescription, though monetarily expensive for the native, has been very accurate and effective tool in the hands of a qualified astrologer.

Logically, some of the gemstones interfere with the cosmic effects of other gems also and thus are in conflict. Under such circumstances, this dynamic prescription of gemstones is very useful as the astrologer can derive benefits for the native from various gemstones at different points of time, without any negative effect of the conflict of gems.

The table below will give the general conflict existing between various gems and the planetary reasons for this astrologically. A competent person, however, can take liberty of prescribing combined gemstones also. Sometimes, it has been seen that the position of planets in the horoscope also shows that combination of certain gemstones would conflict. Thus, a qualified astrologer's opinion should always be sought in wearing more than one gemstone.

Planet	Conflicting Gemstones
SUN	Sun is incompatible with Saturn, Venus, Rahu and Ketu. The gems for Sun like Ruby and Garnet should not be used with Blue Sapphire, Diamond, Hessonite and Cat's Eye.
MOON	Moon is incompatible with Rahu and Ketu. Hence, Moon gems as Pearl, Moonstone should not be prescribed with Hessonite and Cat's Eye.
JUPITER	Jupiter is incompatible with Mercury and Venus.So, Jupiter gems like Yellow Sapphire should not be used with Emerald or Diamond.
RAHU	Rahu is incompatible with Sun and Moon.Rahu gems like Hessonite should not be used with Ruby or Pearl.
KETU	Ketu is incompatible with Sun and Moon.Ketu gems like Cat's Eye should not be used with Ruby or Pearl.
MERCURY	As Mercury is incompatible with Moon, Mercury gems such as Emerald should not be used with Pearl or Moonstone.
VENUS	Venus is incompatible with the Sun and Moon.Hence, Venus gems like Diamond should not be used with Ruby or Pearl.
SATURN	Saturn is incompatible with Sun, Moon and Mars. Saturn gems such as Blue Sapphire should not be used with Ruby, Pearl or Red Coral.
MARS	Mars is incompatible with Mercury and Saturn. Mars gems like Red Coral should not be used with Emerald and Blue Sapphire.

This conflict of gemstones has to be always kept in mind. In order to explain how it works, we discuss below two cases.

The first case is the chart (Chart-F) of another IAS officer who worked in the Government of India in an important Ministry. He came in contact with the author in a conference through a common colleague. He had problems in managing his expenses and felt that he was not able to manage despite best efforts. The said officer has good knowledge of astrology himself. He was advised to wear Cat's eye as Ketu in 12th house of expenses was causing this problem and he was running Ketu dasa also. In addition, he was also asked by the astrologer to wear a Ruby for the lifetime benefits of health and career. His problems persisted and he found no relief.

When he asked the author about this, he was asked to remove the Cat's eye as it conflicts with Ruby and both gems were ineffective. After about one month, the officer met the author and explained that things are improving though Ketu dasa was still running. He also told that in some of the career related matters, he has started finding favours of superiors forthcoming.

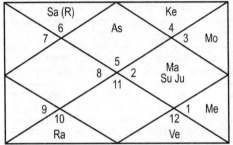

Chart of an IAS officer (Chart-F)

Readers would see that Sun is lagna lord and is placed in 10th house of career. Due to cat's eye interfering, Ruby was also ineffective. After removal of Cat's eye, Ruby's effects leading to 10th house benefits started manifesting even in Ketu dasa

Another chart (Chart-G) shown here is of an IFS (foreign Service) officer. He was posted in India but after 2 years got posted abroad again. He did not want to go out of India. He was under stress and his superiors were not helping him. On the advice of some astrologer, he had put on Hessonite. He was already wearing a Ruby for the last 15 years.

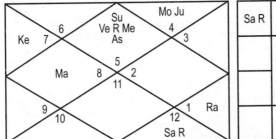
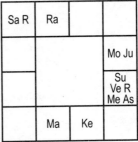

Chart of IFS officer (Chart-G)

When he contacted the author, he was asked to remove Hessonite immediately. Hessonite conflicts with Ruby and renders it corrupt and ineffective. Though, his horoscope is very strong, yet Ruby's benefits were not available to him. His bosses were not listening to him leave aside supporting him to get a change of posting. After removing Hessonite, within a month he could convince his bosses to allow him to be in India for some more period and later has got posting changed to India itself.

The above cases show that the conflict of gemstones should be taken into account very seriously by both layman and practicing astrologers. We can see many people wearing 3 or 4 rings with gemstones prescribed to them at various points of time. They may have conflicting gems. In such cases, wearer requires a prescription to remove some of the gemstones.

Chapter 6

Wearing Gemstones

Principles of wearing Gemstones:

The gemstones are very powerful medium and their effects can be magical as well as very rapid. But this is only possible when these are properly prescribed and are worn by the user in a prescribed manner. Although one can study and learn the use of gemstones from any book or text, but in practice a qualified person should only prescribe the gemstones. Any gemstone when prescribed for a native enhances positively certain aspects of the life but simultaneously gives negative effect on other areas of life also. To understand these pros and cons of any gemstones, one should have proficiency in astrology in addition to the knowledge of the gems and their effects. Only when positive influence of a gem outweighs the negative influence of the gem, it is prescribed.

Sometimes, dynamic prescription of the gems is also done. This system of prescribing gems involves continuous monitoring of the transits of various planets for the native and the changes in Dasas and antardasas of various planets. This is a complicated system and is actually beyond the understanding of persons who are not qualified in astrology. But there are many instances, where it has worked very well for natives over very long periods of time.

Gemstones are worn after prescription. There are means of testing of gemstones before these are prescribed for prolonged use. Also it is very important to know, where it is most beneficial to wear the gemstone. Gemstones work on the usage of their inherent power of transferring energy after filtering. This means that the size and weight of the gemstones are also very important.

Where to wear gemstones:

This is a question, which is very often asked by people and is even debated between astrologers. Some of the astrologers are of the opinion that the gemstones should be worn on fingers in rings, whereas some prescribe them in the form of lockets and amulets.

The argument in favour of lockets is that the gems are away from public gaze and they do not undergo wear and tear. Thus, the properties of the gem remain intact. Also the gem does not come in contact with filth as no one touches it. Another argument is that if a native uses locket, then he experiences a *Ratna Snan* whenever he takes bath. It is said that this is very auspicious. Moreover, if combination of gems is used then it is very easy to make a locket and wear them.

The wearing of gemstones in the form of rings is widely popular and many astrologers have felt that their efficacy is very high when worn in the form of rings. Their argument is that the gems worn in the form of a locket do touch the skin but they are not effective in transferring the sun energy to the body as they are covered by clothes. In ancient times, people used to wear only lower clothes and for upper region they used to wear only a piece of cloth around the neck, which is more like a *stole* of modern day. The shirt like clothes was not used at all. Hence, in those conditions wearing of gems in lockets worked equally well as these were never covered. In those times armlets and amulets studded with gems were also popular as these places were also exposed and were equally beneficial. But in today's times, the rings are the best way of wearing gemstones. An added benefit is that they act as ornaments also, in addition to providing benefits.

Further, the lockets do not come in contact with any nerve endings. But the fingers are having definite nerve endings and these are very sensitive points. This is recognized by medical science also and these nerve endings are used in many other healing systems like acupuncture, acupressure etc. This gives a logical reason for prescribing wearing of gemstones on fingers.

Sine the purpose of wearing a gemstone is to channelise the energy to a person through the medium of Gemstone; hence, wearing it on a finger seems to be a better way. With this the nerve endings come into use and the cosmic energy via the medium of a gemstone gets transferred to the native very effectively. This gives very fast and effective results relating to the effects of the planet associated with the Gemstone.

Selection of Finger for Gemstones:

Each finger has connection with different parts of our body by way of nerves. These intimate connections are the carriers of the filtered energy of gems to those areas and to the body in general to give the required effects. This is also the basis of healing through gems. These fingers are very important from the point of view of gems, which are prescribed. Also fingers have been associated with various planets. These connections are described in the Science of Palmistry and have logical basis for it. It would be inappropriate to discuss Palmistry here. The use of various fingers for specific purpose is explained here.

- *First finger (Tarjani):*

    This finger is also called the index finger or the forefinger. It is under the control of planet Jupiter. Medically, it stands for Respiratory system and the stomach. For curing the disease of the respiratory system, lungs, etc. gems prescribed are worn on this finger. Gems for the Mars and Jupiter are generally worn on this finger. Sometimes stone for Moon is also worn here for specific purpose. Yellow Sapphire, Red Coral work very well on this finger.

- *Second finger (Madhyama):*

    This is generally the longest finger and is also called the middle finger, though it is not the middle one. This is under the direct control of Saturn. Medically, it stands for intestines, mind, brain, liver, and mental structure. Since Rahu astrologically behaves like Saturn, hence, stones for Rahu are also worn on this finger. Gems for Mercury and Venus are also sometimes worn here, as these planets are friends of Saturn. Blue Sapphire is highly powerful on this finger.

- *Third finger (Anamika):*

    This is also called the ring finger because the wedding ring in the western culture is traditionally worn on this finger. Ironically, this finger controls the generative organs! It is also controlling Kidneys, Stomach and blood circulation. The finger is ruled by Sun and it stands for the happier side of the life. Gems for Sun and Mars are worn on this finger. Since Ketu astrologically behaves like Mars, hence, its stone is also worn here.

- **Fourth finger (Kanishtha):**

    This is also called the small finger and is under the direct control of
    Mercury. Medically, it represents private parts, knees, legs and feet.
    For the cure of the diseases of lower parts of the body, gems are
    worn on this finger. Gems for Saturn and Rahu can also be worn
    here, as they are friends of Mercury. Stones for Moon are worn
    here and are very powerful as Moon is great friend of Mercury.

Wearing Gems on Finger:

There is a good deal of confusion prevailing in the minds of people
and even in the minds of some astrologers regarding the technique of
wearing gemstones in fingers. Some of them are firmly of the opinion
that the gems should be placed in the ring in such a manner that it
touches the skin. Others do not bother for such things. There are
some astrologers who actually do not bother to prescribe the correct
way of making rings. Many times the incorrect studding of gems leads
to no effects being felt by the native even after wearing the prescribed
gems. Some people have been found wearing rings where the gemstone
touches the skin and it made a wound on the finger!

Let us rest all this confusion now for the benefit of everybody.
Foremost is the fact that wearing a gemstone is not touch therapy. It
actually is a very scientific technique by using the rays as energised
through the medium of the gemstone. The best way of making the
ring is to leave the hind side of the ring uncovered. This leaves the gem
to work efficiently and the skin directly below is exposed to the filtered
rays. These rays then sensitise the nerve endings and the blood vessels
and the flowing blood carries the effect throughout the body creating
the desired effects. Thus, the prescription of stone touching the skin is
unfounded and unnecessary.

Right weight of the Gemstone:

There is another very important area of gemstone prescription,
which requires certain facts to be enunciated clearly. Classical astrologers
have been using certain thumb rules of prescribing the appropriate
weight of the gems. These astrologers rely upon the knowledge passed
down to them from their teachers and they use it very effectively also.
But even these prescriptions were devised on some principles. Many of

these have been lost. Some of the prescriptions are empirical and are absolutely reliable and accurate.

Another area of sizing the gems for prescription purpose is on the basis of the degrees of the related planet in a sign where it is posited. But a planet can have 30th degree in a sign. Shall we prescribe a stone for that planet in caratage in proportion to the degree in the sign? Similar issue arises when the degree of a planet in a sign is 1st. Using this system is impractical. The gems also work effectively beyond a threshold limit of their size. Below that threshold, they are good for ornamental purpose rather than astrological effects. Many people wear diamond rings with 9 diamonds studded, but they do not get any positive or negative effect. The reason being that the weight of all these diamonds is below the threshold and can not have any effect on the native.

This threshold value for all the stones except Diamond is 4.25 carats and above which is same as 5.25 ratti as per old system of measurement. The Diamond can be 1 carat and above to be effective. The table given below provides a thumb rule about the weights of various popularly used stones and the recommended metal for studding them. It is based on experience and has proved to be highly effective.

The above values of 4.25 carat or 5.25 Ratti is in keeping with the system of "SAVAYA" meaning system of one quarter. In this method any stone, which is prescribed, has to weigh in full weight plus one quarter as well. Diamond is the only stone, which is prescribed out of this savaya system. The system has empirical reasoning behind it and we must subscribe to it as it has been tested over centuries and the gemstones have given effective results in this system.

The conversion table for various weighing systems for gemstones is:

1 Gram = 5 Carats = 1000 Milligrams

200 Milligrams = 1 Carat or = 100 Cents

182 Milligrams = 1 Standard Ratti (Stones Ratti)

121 Milligrams = 1 Sunari Ratti = (Kachhi Ratti)

1 Tola = 11.664 Grams

It is advisable if the stones are bought as per their weight in Carats as it is a standard term throughout the world. But in India, many times you get stones made following the system of Savaya and sold in their weight as Rattis. This should also be acceptable.

Gemstone	Weight	Metal
Ruby	3 To 4 Rattis+ ¼ Ratti	Gold
Pearl	5 To 7 Rattis+ ¼ Ratti	Silver
Red Coral	6 To 10 Rattis+ ¼ Ratti	Gold or Iron
Emerald	4 To 6 Rattis+ ¼ Ratti	Gold
Yellow Sapphire	4 To 5 Rattis+ ¼ Ratti	Gold
Diamond	1 To 4 Rattis+ ¼ Ratti	Gold or Platinum
Blue Sapphire	3 To 4 Rattis+ ¼ Ratti	Silver or Lead
Hessonite	4 To 6 Rattis+ ¼ Ratti	Iron/Alloy
Cat's Eye	2 To 4 Rattis+ ¼ Ratti	Steel or Gold or Alloy

Astrological testing of Gemstones:

The gemstones are tested before being worn by a native to find out whether it is suitable for the native or not. There are various techniques described on the basis of folklore or tradition for testing of gems. These are used by many astrologers even today very frequently. Most of these techniques are rudimentary in nature. The most widely used method is to keep the prescribed stone wrapped in a piece of cloth and kept under the pillow for 7 days. The colour of the cloth varies with the type of stone. If the native does not experience any bad dream or he experiences good dreams, then he is asked to wear it permanently.

Another system used is that the stone is wrapped in the cloth and worn on the upper arm (bicep). If nothing untoward happens, or good things happen, then they are asked to continue the use. Similarly some other techniques are practiced by astrologers in various parts based on local traditions.

Both these practices have no scientific basis at all. In all these techniques, the stones are covered with cloth; hence the sun energy cannot be transmitted. Moreover, the stones take their own time to affect the native. Keeping it near the pillow or on the arm for few days cannot be used as a method to decide the efficacy of a gemstone. It is only very rare that the stone is very powerful for a particular native depending on the dasa running and the position of various planets in the horoscope and gives the effect instantly.

The best way out is that the stone should be tested by actually wearing it. If the ill effects are experienced, then the astrologer should be consulted. If the astrologer is competent, then he will already know these effects. He actually has to balance between the negative and the positive effects of a stone in such a way that the positive things outweigh and native is benefited. Sometimes, the negative effects of a stone can be counter weighed by using another stone in combination as per the horoscope indications and the dasa and antardasas effects. This gives rise to combination stones.

Combination Stones:

It has been experienced that many times after a gem is prescribed after due considerations, it does not give desired results or gives adverse results. There can be many reasons for this.

- The gem has been prescribed in wrong mahadasa and antardasa.

- The gem has given boost to those areas of horoscope where the connected planet aspects and are negative in nature.

- The gem is concerned with a planet, which is part of a wrong yoga in horoscope.

These reasons are just illustrative. There can be many other reasons. Many times even a competent astrologer is not aware of some of the areas, which are influenced by a particular planet for a native, and the effect of a particular yoga in the horoscope and the effect of a gem connected to the planet placed in that yoga. This is the reason that the dynamic prescription is very important. This system takes action to minimize the adverse effects by prescribing some other stone to overshadow the ill effects. This is called combination stones.

The combination stones are also prescribed to give boost to certain good yogas present in the horoscope. Some times Raj yogas present in a horoscope are dormant. They can be made active by using combination gems for the planets involved in the yoga. Similarly, *DHANYOGAS* and other auspicious yogas can also be activated.

In practice, very few astrologers are using this combination stone prescription. But a well conversant astrologer uses them liberally for those people who consult him regularly. In this system, many times the stone for a weak planet can also be used in combination with other stones and the results can be remarkable. The reason being that the effects of the weak planet stones are also good for certain areas of horoscope. Only the ill effects on some areas of life affected by that stone have to be overshadowed with combination gems. These principles can only be put to effective use only after a deep analysis of the birth chart of a native. Further, such use of gemstones should be regularly monitored as well to derive maximum benefits from it.

Wearing Gemstones (Ascendant wise analysis):

We will discuss the effects of nine precious stones corresponding to the nine planets and what are their effects for each ascendant. It gives a basic thumb rule as to which Gemstones are prohibited for some ascendants. Though, the position of the planet corresponding to a particular gemstone has to be taken into account but this discussion will give certain rules, which can guide the readers to understand the basic theory used while prescribing the Gemstones.

RUBY:

1. Aries:

For Aries ascendant, Sun becomes the lord of 5th house which is a Trikona and Sun is a friend of Ascendant lord Mars as well. Since 5th house represents intellect and progeny, hence, wearing Ruby will give the native of Aries ascendant higher intellect, ability to gain higher knowledge, pleasure from children and satisfaction from them. It will also give native support from governmental authorities and superiors in his profession. This will give very good benefits during the Sun period for such a native.

2. Taurus:

For Taurus native Sun is the lord of 4th house but Sun is an enemy of the ascendant lord Venus. Such natives should only wear Ruby during Sun Dasa and should not wear it during other periods as it can give ill effects. Sun favourably placed for Taurus ascendant can be helped by

Ruby to give the native gains of property and vehicles, mental peace and good family life as well.

3. Gemini:

For Gemini native, Sun is the lord of 3rd house. This is a Dusthana and such natives should not wear Ruby, as it will prove harmful for the native.

4. Cancer:

For Cancer natives, Sun is the lord of 2nd house which is house of funds. Sun is also a friend of Moon the ascendant lord. Hence, if these natives face financial problems, they should wear Ruby. If these natives face eye problems, then also they can wear Ruby. Since Sun is lord of marak house here, hence it is advisable to wear Ruby along with white Pearl for these natives.

5. Leo:

Here Sun is lord of the ascendant. Hence for these natives, Ruby is birthstone and is very beneficial. These natives can wear a Ruby for life. Ruby will protect the person against illnesses and enemies of all types. Since Leo natives can be emotional, Ruby helps them in maintaining mental and nerve control and also increases the self-confidence.

6. Virgo:

For these natives, since Sun is the lord of 12th house, these natives should never wear Ruby, as it will be extremely harmful for them.

7. Libra:

For Libra native, Sun is the lord of 11th house of gains. But Sun is also an enemy of Venus, the ascendant lord. Thus, it is advisable for these natives to wear Ruby only during the Dasa of Sun to get gains. Otherwise, these natives should avoid wearing Ruby.

8. Scorpio:

For Scorpio natives, Sun is the lord of 10th house of profession and career. This is a Kendra house also and Sun can prove Rajyoga Karaka for these natives. Sun is also friend of Lagna lord Mars here. These natives can wear Ruby and will get promotions in career, access to superior authorities, name and fame and such beneficial effects in profession. Ruby can help these natives to the extreme in Sun mahadasa.

9. Sagittarius:

In this case Sun becomes the lord of 9th house which is a Trikona and again it can be yogakaraka. Here also Sun is friend of the lagna lord Jupiter. Hence, Ruby if worn by such native will bring good opportunities in life for the native. Wearing it can help the father of the native as well. The effects will be pronounced in the mahadasa of Sun.

10. Capricorn:

In this case Sun is lord of the 8th house of death. Sun is also enemy of Lagna lord Saturn. Hence, these Capricorn ascendant natives should never wear ruby, as it will give them death like sufferings.

11. Aquarius:

In such case Sun is the lord of 7th house of marriage and partnerships. Here Sun acquires marak propensity and it is enemy of Lagna lord Saturn. Such natives should never wear Ruby, as it will give them sufferings.

12. Pisces:

Here Sun is lord of 6th house which is a Dusthana. But Sun here is friend of Lagna lord Jupiter. These natives should not wear Ruby as a general rule. But one exception is there. If Sun here is placed in 6th house itself in birth chart, then during Sun dasa Ruby will give extreme beneficial effects, as it will enhance the effects of own house placement.

WHITE PEARL

1. Aries:

For Aries ascendant Moon becomes the lord of 4th house which is a Kendra house and Moon is a friend of Ascendant lord Mars as well. Since 4th house represents property, mother, family happiness and vehicles, hence, wearing Pearl will help the native in these matters. This can prove extremely beneficial in Moon mahadasa. Pearl gives lot of mental peace and stability. If Red coral is worn along with the Pearl, then it will prove very beneficial to these natives.

2. Taurus:

For Taurus native Moon is the lord of 3rd house, these natives should never wear Pearl, as it will have adverse effect in general.

3. Gemini:

For Gemini native, Moon is the lord of 2nd house. The native can wear Pearl in Moon mahadasa, but it has to be carefully assessed. Moon is lord of a Marak place here and Pearl can give troubles also. If Moon is in 2nd, 9th, 10th or 11th house here, then only Pearl can be worn in its Mahadasa.

4. Cancer:

For Cancer natives, Moon is the lord of ascendant. These natives can wear Pearl for life. This will protect their health and increases the longevity. These natives will have protection for funds also if Pearl is worn. Pearl will also enhance the personality and outlook of such natives and stability of thoughts is also achieved.

5. Leo:

Moon here is lord of 12th house and it is a Dusthana. These natives should not wear Pearl. Only if Moon is in 12th house, then during Moon dasa, Pearl can be beneficial, as it will enhance the own house placement in the horoscope.

6. Virgo:

Here for such natives, Moon is lord of 11th house of gains. If Pearl is worn during the Dasa of Moon, it gives very good material gains and desires start getting fulfilled also. Here pearl also helps in begetting progeny and fame also.

7. Libra:

For Libra native, Moon is the lord of 10th house of profession. Though the Lagna lord Venus and Moon are not friends, yet wearing a Pearl will benefit the native in getting help from superior authorities, name and fame and status. The progress in career is triggered and if the Moon dasa operates, then extreme beneficial results are achieved.

8. Scorpio:

For Scorpio natives, Moon is the lord of 9th house which is a Trikona house. Moon can be yogakaraka for such natives. Moon and lagna lord Mars are friends as well. Wearing Pearl will give the native very good opportunities to get progress in material as well as spiritual life. Here it will help the native's father as well.

9. Sagittarius:

In this case Moon is lord of 8th house of death. These natives should never wear a Pearl.

10. Capricorn:

For these natives, Moon is lord of 7th house which is a Marak house. Moon is enemy of Saturn also which is lagna lord. These natives should not wear Pearl at all.

11. Aquarius:

Here Moon is lord of 6th house. Moon is enemy of lagna lord Saturn as well. These natives should never wear a Pearl.

12. Pisces:

Moon in this case is lord of the 5th house which is a Trikona house as well. Pearl if worn by such natives can give progeny to the native. It helps the person get higher education and name fame as well. Happiness from children is also available for such natives. It helps the material gains as well especially during the Dasa of Moon.

RED CORAL

1. Aries:

In this case Mars is the Lagna lord. These natives can wear Red Coral for life. It gives them robust physique, protection from diseases, name and fame. It gives enhancement of personality and general prosperity.

2. Taurus:

These natives have Mars as lord of 12th house and 7th house. Both are not good and these natives are advised never to wear a Red Coral.

3. Gemini:

In these cases, Mars becomes the lord of 11th house and 6th house. These natives should also not wear Red Coral except in cases where Mars is in 11th or 6th house itself. In such case, Red Coral should be worn only during Mars Dasa period and should be removed after that. Generally, these natives should avoid wearing Red Coral.

4. Cancer:

For Cancer natives, Mars is the lord of 10th house and 5th house. Here Mars is yogakaraka for the natives. They should wear it for life. This will give them name, Fame, happiness from children, begetting children, progress in profession, help of superior authorities as well. Since Mars is friend of Lagna lord Moon, these natives should wear Pearl and Red Coral together to derive extremely beneficial results. For female natives, wearing Red Coral gives them very good results as far as married life is concerned.

5. Leo:

Here Mars is lord of 9th house and 4th house and is again yogakaraka for these natives. Red Coral will give property and vehicles. It will also enhance the status of the native. Red coral will prove beneficial for mother of the native and will also get opportunities in life for the native.

6. Virgo:

For these natives, since Mars is the lord of 3rd and 8th house which are both dusthanas. These natives should never wear Red Coral, as it will be extremely harmful for them.

7. Libra:

Here Mars is lord of 2nd house and 7th house. It acquires Marak propensities. These natives should never wear Red Coral as it can give death also. If the native is in such an age and birth chart shows long life, even then it can give death like suffering.

8. Scorpio:

For Scorpio natives, Mars is the lord of ascendant and 6th house. Though 6th house is a Dusthana but being Lagna lord, it will be benefic for the natives. These natives can wear Red Coral for life.

9. Sagittarius:

Mars in this case is lord of 12th house and 5th house. Mars is considered to be a beneficial planet for these natives, as it owns 5th house. Red coral will give progeny and happiness from children. It also helps in skill up gradation and higher education of the native.

10. Capricorn:

Here Mars is lord of 11th house and 4th house. Red Coral can be worn during Mars Dasa. It will help the native in property related matters and gains from it. It can help in acquiring good vehicles and also material gains in life.

11. Aquarius:

Here Mars becomes lord of 3rd house and 10th house. These natives should not wear Red Coral unless Mars is in 10th house. Even then only during Mars dasa Red Coral is advised to get benefits in profession and support of authorities.

12. Pisces:

Mars is lord of 2nd house and 9th house and is considered very beneficial for Pisces ascendant. These natives should wear Red Coral. They will get benefits in getting opportunities in life. Wearing Yellow Sapphire with it will help the native in getting extremely good benefits.

EMERALD

1. Aries:

The lord of Emerald is Mercury and Mercury for these natives owns two houses 3rd and 6th house. Both these houses are dusthanas. Thus, these natives should not wear Emerald at all.

2. Taurus:

Mercury here owns 2nd house and 5th house and becomes a very beneficial planet here. If Emerald is worn, then it will give peace, financial gains, and happiness from progeny. During Mercury period, it proves extremely beneficial. If these natives wear Emerald and Diamond together, then they can be financially very prosperous in life.

3. Gemini:

For these natives, Mercury is lord of Lagna and 4th house. Mercury is yogakaraka for these natives. Emerald should be worn by these natives for life as it works as a protection for life. Wearing this will give property and vehicle benefits and also opportunities in life. This imparts mercurial benefits to the personality of the native.

4. Cancer:

Mercury owns two Dusthana i.e. 12th house and 3rd house. These natives should never wear Emerald. as it will be harmful for them.

5. Leo:

For these natives, Mercury is the lord of 11th house of gains and 2nd house of funds. These natives should wear Emerald only during the dasa of Mercury and they will get financial benefits and family happiness along with name and fame.

6. Virgo:

Here Mercury is the Lagna lord and lord of 10th house. It becomes yogakaraka. These natives should wear Emerald for life. It will protect health and also gives career benefits. In Mercury Dasa, extremely beneficial results will be experienced.

7. Libra:

Mercury for these natives is lord of 12 th and 9th houses. Mercury is considered a beneficial planet for these natives. These natives should wear Emerald along with Diamond. They will get fortunate openings in life due to its effects.

8. Scorpio:

Mercury for these natives owns 8th and 11th house. Mars as lagna lord and Mercury are enemies. These natives should avoid wearing Emerald. But if Mercury is placed in 2nd, 4th, 5th, 9th or 11th house, then Emerald can be worn during dasa of mercury only and should be removed after that. This will give good financial gains in such cases.

9. Sagittarius:

Mercury here is lord of two Kendras i.e. 7th and 10th house. It suffers from Kendradhipati Dosha. Emerald should be avoided. It can be worn if Mercury is placed in 2nd, 5th, 9th, 10th or 11th house in birth chart. Here Emerald will give financial benefits during its Dasa period.

10. Capricorn:

For these natives, Mercury is lord of 6th and 9th houses. Its Mooltrikona sign falls in 9th house. Hence, it is considered beneficial for these natives. Mercury is friend of Lagna lord Saturn. Emerald should be worn with Blue Sapphire here. In Mercury dasa, wearing Emerald will give very beneficial effects.

11. Aquarius:

Here Mercury is friend of Lagna lord Saturn and owns 8th and 5th houses. It is considered beneficial for these natives. These people can wear Emerald during Dasa of Mercury Combining it with yogakaraka Venus Gem of Diamond can give added benefits.

12. Pisces:

Mercury here owns 4th and 7th houses and suffers from Kendradhipati Dosha. But if Mercury is posited in 2nd, 5th, 9th, 10th or 11th houses of horoscope, then Emerald will prove beneficial for material benefits during its dasa.

YELLOW SAPPHIRE

1. Aries:

Jupiter lords over this stone and here Jupiter owns 12th house and 9th house. Since it owns a Trikona house, it is a beneficial planet for these natives. These natives get wisdom, intellect, sagacity of thought and advancement in fortune and opportunities after wearing Yellow Sapphire. They will get extremely good results during the Dasa of Jupiter and if worn along with Red Coral.

2. Taurus:

Here Jupiter owns 8th and 11th houses. It is not considered to be a beneficial planet for this ascendant. Moreover, lagna lord Venus and Jupiter are not friends. These people should not wear Yellow Sapphire. But if Jupiter is placed in 2nd, 4th, 5th, 9th or lagna then this stone can give material benefits but should be worn only during its Dasa.

3. Gemini:

For these natives, Jupiter owns 7th and 10th houses. It suffers from Kendradhipati Dosha. These people should avoid wearing Yellow Sapphire. Even then if Jupiter is placed in Lagna, 2nd house, and 11th house or in a Trikona house, then during Dasa of Jupiter Yellow Sapphire can be worn. It will give progenic happiness, material benefits but caution has to be observed as it is maraka as well.

4. Cancer:

Here Jupiter is lord of 6th and 9th houses. It is considered beneficial for the natives. Hence, if these natives wear Yellow Sapphire, then they will get progenic happiness, growth in intellect, name and status and material benefits. If Red Coral is also worn with it, then added benefits accrue to the native.

5. Leo:

Here Jupiter becomes lord of 5th house which is Trikona house and 8th house of death. Since it owns 5th house, it is considered beneficial. Wearing Yellow Sapphire for these natives is very beneficial. If worn with Ruby, then much better results are experienced.

6. Virgo:

For these natives, Jupiter owns 4th and 7th houses. Here it suffers from Kendradhipati Dosha. It is marak lord also. These natives should avoid wearing Yellow Sapphire. But if Jupiter is posited in the birth chart in 2nd, 4th, 5th, 7th, 9th, 10th or 11th house, then wearing Yellow Sapphire will bring status, sagacity, progenic happiness and material benefits.

7. Libra:

For Libra native, Jupiter is the lord of 3rd and 6th houses both dusthanas. These natives should not wear yellow Sapphire.

8. Scorpio:

For Scorpio natives, Jupiter owns 2nd and 5th houses. Here it is very beneficial. These natives should wear Yellow Sapphire. Moreover, Mars and Jupiter are friends. This will benefit materially and funds position gets a boost here in addition to improving the intellect of the native.

9. Sagittarius:

For these natives, Jupiter owns Lagna and 4th house. Here it becomes Yogakaraka and extremely beneficial. These persons should wear Yellow Sapphire for life. It will act like a shelter for these natives. During the Dasa of Jupiter it will give landed property and vehicles and will improve the status of individual. If worn with a Ruby, then added benefits will accrue to native.

10. Capricorn:

For these natives, Jupiter owns 12th and 3rd house and is not beneficial at all. They should never wear yellow Sapphire.

11. Aquarius:

Here Jupiter owns 2nd and 11th houses. Lagna lord Saturn is enemy of Jupiter. Even then during the period of Jupiter, Yellow Sapphire can be worn. It gives material benefits, progenic happiness, improvements in education and intellect. But it is Maraka lord as well so caution has to be observed by these natives while using Yellow Sapphire.

12. Pisces:

Here Jupiter owns Lagna and 10th house. It is yogakaraka and gives good results. Yellow sapphire by these natives should be worn for life. If Red Coral is also worn, then added benefits can be felt. It will give good career benefits to such natives.

DIAMOND

1. Aries:

For Aries ascendant Venus, which is lord of Diamond, owns 2nd and 7th houses. Both are marak places and it acquires marak propensities. Moreover, lagna lord Mars and Venus both are not friends. Thus, these natives should never wear Diamond.

2. Taurus:

Venus here becomes Lagna lord and lord of 8th house. These natives can wear Diamond for life and will get lot of protection, enhancement in beauty and personality. Marital harmony, happy married life, vehicle benefits and all sorts of luxuries will be available to these natives.

3. Gemini:

For Gemini native, Venus is lord of 12th house and 5th house. 5th house has Mooltrikona sign of Venus and lagna lord is friend of Venus. These natives get lot of benefits if they wear Diamond. General prosperity, progenic happiness, status and access to luxuries are ensured after wearing Diamond.

4. Cancer:

For Cancer natives, Venus is the lord of 4th house and 11th house. Venus is considered a bad planet for Cancer ascendant. Lagna lord Moon and Venus are not friendly. Only during Venus dasa, Diamond can be worn as 4th and 11th houses are good houses.

5. Leo:

Venus is not considered beneficial planet as it owns 3rd and 10th house. But during Venus dasa, Diamond can be worn. It is best if these natives avoid wearing Diamond.

6. Virgo:

Here Venus owns 2nd and 9th houses. It is considered very beneficial planet. Hence, wearing Diamond will give all round progress to these natives. Wearing Emerald along with it is added benefit.

7. Libra:

For Libra native, Venus owns Lagna. These natives can wear Diamond for life. This will give them protection from ill health and will add charm to their personality. It helps in longevity, status and name during the period of Venus.

8. Scorpio:

For Scorpio natives, Venus is lord of 12th house and 7th house. The lagna lord Mars is not friendly with Venus. These natives should never wear Diamond.

9. Sagittarius:

Here Venus lords over 6th and 11th houses. It is not considered a beneficial planet for these natives. Even then, if Venus is posited in 2nd, 4th, 5th, 9th, 11th or in its own sign, then during Venus dasa one can wear Diamond. Here it will give material benefits.

10. Capricorn:

In this case Venus is lord of 5th and 10th house. It becomes yogakaraka planet. These people can wear Diamond and it will give intellectual advancement, progress in career and benefits from superiors to these natives. If worn with Blue Sapphire, then it can give phenomenal results to these natives.

11. Aquarius:

In this case Venus becomes lord of 4th and 9th house. It is again yogakaraka planet here. These natives can wear Diamond and it will give them huge material benefits along with some great opportunities in life. If worn with Blue Sapphire, the results will get magnified.

12. Pisces:

Venus here is the lord of 3rd and 8th houses. Both these houses are bad and Venus does not give good results. These natives should avoid wearing Diamond.

BLUE SAPPHIRE

1. Aries:

For Aries ascendant, Saturn becomes the lord of 10th and 11th houses. Both are good houses but ownership of 11th house has not been considered good for these natives. Even then Saturn in 2nd, 4th, 5th, 9th, 10th, 11th houses or Lagna will give beneficial results during Dasa of Saturn. Blue Sapphire in such cases can be worn only during Saturn Dasa.

2. Taurus:

For Taurus native Saturn is lord of 9th and 10th houses. Here it becomes yogakaraka. If these natives wear Blue Sapphire, then they will always be prosperous, acquire status, material benefits and prosperity. It can be worn with Diamond by such persons to derive even better results.

3. Gemini:

For Gemini native, Saturn is lord of 8th and 9th houses. It is considered beneficial as it owns 9th house here. Blue Sapphire can be worn by these natives along with Emerald for benefit. Saturn dasa is the best time to wear Blue Sapphire.

4. Cancer:

For Cancer natives, Saturn owns 7th house and 8th house. 7th is marak house and 8th house is of death. Saturn is not considered a good planet for these natives. They should never wear Blue Sapphire.

5.   Leo:

Here Saturn owns 6th and 7th house. Both are not good places. These natives should never wear Blue Sapphire.

6.   Virgo:

Saturn here owns 5th house and 6th house. Since it owns 5th house, it is not bad for such natives. But these persons should wear Blue Sapphire only during the dasa of Saturn.

7.   Libra:

Saturn owns for such natives both 4th and 5th houses. Here it is yogakaraka planet. It is extremely beneficial. These natives should wear Blue Sapphire for material benefits, fixed assets and gains from then. Saturn is friend of Venus, the lagna lord, as well. Here it will give very good benefits to the native if Diamond is also worn along with Blue Sapphire.

8.   Scorpio:

For these natives, Saturn owns 3rd and 4th houses. It is not considered a good planet for these persons. They should avoid wearing Blue sapphire. If Saturn is placed in 5th, 9th, 10th or 11th house, only then it can be worn during Saturn dasa.

9.   Sagittarius:

Here Saturn owns a marak house 2nd and 3rd house which is Dusthana. Saturn is malefic for these natives. Saturn is not friendly with Lagna lord Jupiter as well. These natives should not wear Blue Sapphire.

10. Capricorn:

Here Saturn is the owner of Lagna and 2nd house. These natives should wear Blue Sapphire always for prosperity and material benefits.

11. Aquarius:

Here also Saturn is the owner of Lagna and 12th house. For these natives, it gives good results . These people should wear Blue Sapphire for life to get protection from ill health and for general prosperity.

12. Pisces:

For these natives, Saturn is the lord of 11th and 12th houses.. It is considered malefic planet for these natives. Saturn is enemy of lagna lord Jupiter. Even then for material gains, these natives can wear Blue Sapphire during Saturn dasa but it is advisable for these natives to avoid wearing Blue Sapphire as it does more harm than good.

HESSONITE AND CAT'S EYE

These gemstones are for Rahu and Ketu. Both these are shadow planets and do not own any sign of the zodiac. Hence, there are no thumb rules for them. Their prescription is based on analysis and their placement in the birth chart. Moreover, these planets acquire the effects of planets that are in conjunction with them. All this has to be evaluated before prescribing their Gemstones.

Ritual Way of wearing gemstones:

All these nine precious gemstones are very powerful medium. They affect the areas of a native very rapidly. Especially those which are transparent take effect immediately. Thus, any negative energy associated with these gemstones has to be removed before these are worn by the native. These gemstones have their own vibrations which are connected with the colour of the stone and also the connected planet. These stones have to be energised to draw away negative energy from them and to put them into an excited state where they resonate with cosmic energy to give full benefits to the native wearing them. We give below the ritual way of wearing the gemstones. This energising is tedious process and one can ask a learned person to do it for a native. But if the native can recite the Mantra for the Gemstone, then it is best that he himself energises the stone.

RUBY:

Ruby should be worn on a Sunday of bright half (Shukla Paksha) of Moon at the time of Sunrise. Before wearing the ring has to be washed in unboiled milk and holy water. Then it should be worshipped with incense and flowers and the Mantra for Sun should be recited 7000 times.

Om Ghrini Suryaya Namah.

After that the ring should be worn on the ring finger. The same procedure should be adopted while wearing a substitute stone for Ruby. Ruby is best when studded snugly in a Gold ring without claws.

WHITE PEARL:

The ring of Pearl should be made of Silver and can be worn on Monday of the bright half (Shukla Paksha) of Moon. The process of energising it is same and the mantra for Moon is

Om Son Somaye Namah.

The mantra should be recited 11000 times and ring should be worn in the evening in the small finger. The process of energising and worshipping is same for substitute stones for Pearl.

RED CORAL:

Red Coral is studded in Gold. The ring should be worshipped in the same way and the Mantra for Mars should be recited 10000 times. It should be worn in Shukla Paksha Tuesday one hour after Sunrise. The Mantra is

Om Am Aangarkaya Namah.

The process for energising the substitute for Red Coral is same. The ring should be worn in the ring finger.

EMERALD:

Emerald can be studded in gold as well as silver. It is worn on Wednesday of Shukla Paksha 2 hours after sunrise. It should be worn in the little finger after energising. The mantra is

Om Bu Budhaye Namah.

This mantra should be recited 9000 times and ring should be worn after worshipping. The same process is done for substitute stones for Moon as well.

YELLOW SAPPHIRE:

Yellow Sapphire has to be studded in gold. It is worn in Shukla Paksha Thursday. The ring is worn on First finger after energising and worshipping it and is worn one hour before Sunset.. The mantra for Jupiter is

Om Bri Brihaspataye Namah.

The mantra should be recited 19000 times for energising the Gem. The same process is done for energising the substitute Gem for Jupiter.

DIAMOND:

Diamond should be worn in silver or platinum. It also works well in Gold also. The ring is worn on ring finger on Friday of Shukla Paksha in the early morning. It should be energised by reciting the Mantra

Om Shu Shukraye Namah.

This mantra should be recited 19000 times and ring should be worshipped before wearing. The same process is carried out for substitute stones as well.

BLUE SAPPHIRE:

Blue sapphire ring is best in alloy or Panchdhatu or even gold. It should be worshipped and energised. It should be worn in the middle finger on a Saturday of Shukla Paksha 2 hours before sunset. The mantra for Saturn is

Om Shum Shaneyshcharya Namah.

The mantra should be recited 23000 times and ring should be worshipped. Same process should be done for substitute stone.

HESSONITE:

It should be worn in alloy (Ashtadhatu or Steel). Even Silver is very good metal. The ring is worn on a Saturday of Shukla Paksha 2 hrs after Sunset. The mantra for energising the ring is

Om Ran Rahuve Namah.

The mantra should be recited 18000 times and ring should be worshipped. The ring should be worn in middle finger. The same process is used for energising the substitute stones.

CAT'S EYE:

Cat's eye is best in Silver ring. It should be worn on a Tuesday of Shukla Paksha at midnight in the ring finger. The mantra for energising the ring is

Om Ke Ketve Namah.

The ring should be worshipped by reciting the mantra 17000 times and for substitute stones also the same process of energising should be adopted.

Chapter 7

Gemstones for Prosperity and Wealth

Introduction:

Man has always been flummoxed by the fact that there are great disparities between two individual's wealth and prosperity. There are disparities in prosperity of nations even. Wealthy nations also have people who are unfortunate to be paupers. On the other hand the poorer nations have wealthiest of people. This has always been a question in the mind of man as to why it happens. Hard work will make you prosperous. But then many labourers continue to labour whole of their lives without prosperity. It has been seen that wealthiest people turn paupers. Kings getting jailed for years. How does one explain all this? Astrology provides an answer to all this. If your horoscope has activated yoga for wealth and prosperity, then you will prosper. If there are active indications for penury, then kings also live like beggars.

It is beyond any doubt that astrology has satisfied the curiosity of man since ancient times about the question of prosperity and wealth. These days, with the exponential growth of middle class population and growing material consumption trends, this question about money, wealth and prosperity is becoming a matter of ever increasing curiosity. This can be tackled very easily by astrology.

The active yogas for prosperity and wealth undoubtedly give prosperity indicated by them and the position of other planets. But there are many people, where the yogas are present in their horoscopes, but the wealth is missing. Can we excite these yogas to increase the prosperity of a native? The answer is yes we can. The science of gemstones helps us here. Since ancient times, gemstones have been used by mankind for helping them in various matters. They can be used for increasing wealth and prosperity of natives also. But then it can be achieved by understanding the requirements astrologically. This requires a thorough analysis of the birth chart deeply.

The running dasa and antardasa are very important in the case of a native to achieve wealth and prosperity. The yogas present in the horoscope may not give desired results in the dasa of an unfavourable planet. This has to be assessed properly by the astrologer and find out a gemstone, which can help excite the native's yoga for wealth. Sometimes combination stones are very effective in exciting such yogas. The ill effects of dasa can continue but then these gemstones help get some improvements which gives relief to the native.

Gemstones For General prosperity:

The birthstones are generally prescribed for prosperity as they affect the native in a positive manner barring rare instances. This prescription is based on the lord of the ascendant or the lord of Moon sign and the connected stone. This is a general kind of prescription although a slightly better way of prescribing gemstone is on the basis of birth Nakshatra.The effects of the stone for prosperity are discussed below. This discussion is not specific for wealth but for prosperity, which includes all aspects of life like marital felicity, health issues, emotional issues, education and all such things which combined together can be classified as general prosperity. This is only a general way of prescription and for specific remedies about wealth and prosperity issues; a detail analysis of the birth chart has to be done to arrive at appropriate gemstone.

Gemstones and Wealth:

Wealth is an issue about which lot of queries crop up in the minds of people. How much money makes a man wealthy enough? There are no straight answers as this is based on perception of the native also. For a labourer, few lakh rupees may be wealth. But for a businessman, few crore may not be enough. Astrology can help in identifying the presence of combinations of wealth in a native horoscope. These combinations are called *DHAN YOGAS.* Classical treatises on astrology have discussed these combinations very crisply which shows that wealth is an important aspect of astrology. An astrologer can identify the presence or absence of these yogas, then what next? When does these yogas help the native? This question has to be answered. In many cases, it is found that the yogas remain dormant due to the effect of the dasa period of a malefic planet continuing and many times unfavourable yogas are working against the wealth creation for the native.

Gemstones have been used for wealth for ages. In many cases, they have proved immensely beneficial and they excite certain yogas lying dormant for the native. Innumerable instances have been noticed where gemstones have resulted in a deluge of wealth for the native. But for this the astrologer must be highly proficient. The effects of a gemstone are both positive and negative. A particular gemstone can be very useful for wealth in a case, but may help marak propensities. Such gemstones cannot be prescribed. All such aspects have to be taken into consideration before prescribing any gemstone. Many times a yoga (which is formed by more than one planet) is excited using a combination of gemstones. This, if done after proper assessment combination gemstones have been known to override even the evil effects of dasa periods provided other factors are favourable.

Yogas for Great Affluence:

The classical texts have said that if in a horoscope the 5th house lord is in 5th house and the 11th house lord is in 11th house, then the native is bound to get immense wealth. In the case of Taurus and Aquarius ascendant, Mercury be in 5th house and Jupiter in 11th house should have Moon and Mars with it.

In such natives where this yoga is present, wealth in abundance is predicted. These natives can have some setback in their life due to unfavourable dasa and transits but the basic yoga is there in their chart. Such natives can wear gems for the 5th and 11th lord provided the effects are not adverse due to the planet owning a marak or evil house. Mere presence of this yoga actually bestows wealth. The native can have problems in wealth due to unfavourable transits and dasa periods, but these are not severe and can be overcome by using appropriate gemstone. Dynamic prescription of gemstones keeping in view the dasa and transits can be very beneficial for such cases.

Other yogas for great affluence will involve 2nd house and its lord, 11th house and its lord, 9th house and its lord. If there are fortunate yogas or combinations between these planets and they are posited in these very houses or in Kendras or Trikonas without any malefic influence, then great affluence is indicated. Mere presence of these yogas will ensure affluence. But even an affluent person can have bad times. This can be due to malefic transit or Dasa/Antardasa of a malefic planet. But these periods in such cases are only transient and pass away as well. But Gemstones can be prescribed for these periods to help the native. Sometimes, a combination of stones for the planets involved in yoga for affluence can also be prescribed for life if they do not own malefic houses. This keeps the combination of affluence active even if Dasa periods of planets involved are not experienced by native or malefic periods are operating.

Yogas For Wealth:

The yogas for wealth are based on ascendant lord and their combination with other planets conferring wealth on the native. The chart below gives a complete view of these yogas.

Ascendant	Planet in Ascendant	Conjuct with or Aspected by
Leo	Sun	Mars & Jupiter
Cancer	Moon	Mercury & Jupiter
Aries & Scorpio	Mars	Mercury, Venus & Saturn
Gemini & Virgo	Mercury	Saturn & Jupiter
Sagittarius & Pisces	Jupiter	Mercury & Mars
Taurus & Libra	Venus	Saturn & Mercury
Capricorn & Aquarius	Saturn	Mars & Jupiter

In all these yogas the gemstone for the ascendant lord can be prescribed safely as this will be the birthstone as well. During adverse dasa period, other planets, which are a part of the yoga, can be strengthened by prescribing additional stone to give boost to the wealth yoga. Care has to be taken that the stone prescribed may not adversely affect other aspects of life.

In addition, one must wear stone for the planets, which are conjunct, the lord of ascendant, as these planets are a part of the yoga for wealth. The combination stone will be very beneficial, as it will keep the Dhan Yoga active even during unfavourable transits and dasa periods. The prescription should take into account the adverse effects of the gemstones also on other areas of life as per the horoscope of the native.

Another important yoga for wealth and material gains is Chandra Mangal Yoga. In this yoga Moon and Mars are in conjunction. The second case of this yoga is when Moon and Mars are in 7th house from each other meaning they are opposite to each other in a horoscope. The strength of yoga is also dependent upon the placement of both planets in good rashis and houses as well.

This yoga indicates good wealth but the means to make the wealth can be even illegal. If Jupiter has an aspect on the yoga, then the means of making wealth will be legitimate. If this yoga happens to be in 2nd house, 5th house, 9th house, 11th house, then it will give huge amount of wealth to native. This yoga works even if dasa of Moon or Mars is not experienced by the native. Gemstones can help those natives who experience problems in making money during bad Dasa and transits even when they have the presence of this yoga in their charts. Gemstones can help keep this yoga alive and active by prescribing a combination of white Pearl and Red Coral of appropriate weight. This helps the person in maintaining a minimum level of wealth earning even during adverse periods. The only precaution has to be observed that during such bad Dasa, these planets should not be occupying Marak houses or they should not own marak houses.

We will discuss here the case of an Ex- Army officer. He was born on 10th November 1937 at 17:32 hrs. at Khurda in Orissa.

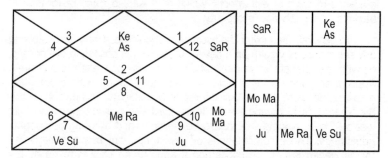

Chart of Native born on 10th Nov. 1937 at Khurda Orissa.

The native joined Army and was working in various capacities. The significant time came when he was posted in ordnance side. He started dealing with the arms suppliers and started making money. Later he quit army and works as middleman for small arms dealers and is very wealthy person. The presence of Chandra Mangal Yoga is manifest here. The means of making money were not legal, but he was not bothered and made money.

He contacted author to predict about his future in politics. This was the time it was observed that he was wearing both Red Coral and

White Pearl. This also made the Chandra Mangal yoga very effective and active.

Gemstones for Other Cases:

Normally, one would come across horoscopes where Dhan yogas are not present. In such cases, the wealth in abundance is not indicated definitely. But then the 9th lord and 5th lord are capable of bestowing wealth. This has been stated even by the great saint Parashara in one of the verses. Thus, if the 5th and 9th lord are well placed in a horoscope, then wealth is indicated. If a favourable planet joins them, then it also becomes a secondary significator for wealth.

During the dasas of 5th or 9th lord, if well placed, wealth will come to the native. These planets can be strengthened by using appropriate gemstones. Even dynamic prescription can be used as long as the dasa of that planet lasts. Later, other gemstones can be prescribed based on the dasa period. When the 5th lord or the 9th lord is not well placed or is not strong in a horoscope, it is very difficult to indicate wealth to the native. The propitiation of that planet should be done under proper guidance to ward of evil effects, which may lead to some restoration of balance of wealth and prosperity.

In general, the lord of the ascendant should be strong for bestowing any semblance of wealth on a native. If this lord is posited in evil houses, or with evil planets or in debilitation, then loss of wealth is indicated. Appropriate gemstones should be prescribed along with propitiation measures to ward off the evil effects of the planets. In addition to this the 5th lord, 9th lord and the 2nd house lord also provide the native with wealth. These planets should also be strengthened by using appropriate gemstones. These combinations of gemstones can help the native as far as wealth issues are concerned if appropriate care is taken by the astrologer while prescribing the gemstones.

Cases with Combination for Penury:

Sage Parashara has described certain combinations, which lead to penury. The essence of these combinations is that the ascendant lord exchanges its house with lord of 6th or 8th or 12th lord and receives aspect from a marak lord. Other combination for penury is when the 5th lord as well as 9th lord are posited in 6th and 12th house respectively.

The combinations of penury definitely affect the wealth of the native. But gemstones have been known to help in these cases. In such cases where the ascendant lord is involved in penury combination, gemstones for 5th lord and 9th lord should be prescribed. Combination stones are best in such cases. If the 5th and 9th lord are aspecting each other, then highly favourable results are experienced. If these two lords are not aspecting but in turn aspect the third planet, then a gemstone combination involving the third planet helps in forming yoga, which can help the native as far as, wealth is concerned. There can be numerous combinations possible and prescription of gems can only be done on individual basis. Moreover, the effect of prescribed Gems on any area of native's life in a negative way must be weighed properly.

There are cases of penury where the 5th and the 9th lord are placed unfavourably. In such cases one should prescribe gemstones for ascendant lord if it is reasonably strong. Simultaneously, propitiation of 5th lord and the 9th lord should be carried out to ward off the evil effects of their placements. In addition any other strong planet can also be strengthened, if it is associated with 9th, 11th or 5th or 2nd house to help native's wealth. All such permutations and combinations can be worked out only after looking into all aspects of horoscope.

Chapter 8

Professions and Gemstones

Introduction:

Man has been baffled by the uncertainty of the future of his life. People have been known to do weird things just to get a glimpse about the coming events in their life, be it career growth, money, professional growth etc. The same was the case with ancients. They were aware of the science of astrology and knew how to predict the future events with remarkable accuracy.

One of the main areas of concern for any person is his profession. The present age is of stiff competition. Naturally, everyone cannot succeed in the chosen field. Sometimes a person suffers serious setback in an otherwise excellent career. People have been known to go to jail while working in powerful positions. This makes everything very uncertain for a common man. Many a times this uncertainty takes a person by total surprise. Is there a solution to this? The answer lies in astrology.

Astrology has been known to provide us deep insights into the kind of profession to pursue and the kind of ups and downs one faces in careers. It can time such ups and downs very accurately. This helps people to be prepared mentally to face such situation of adversity and come out of it also. Another connected issue with this is whether there is any way to prevent such things. Here the use of gemstones comes into picture. They are known to provide certain effects in their own way, which helps the person in his career and profession.

There are many ways where a native can face problems in profession. People who are very successful in their careers can have serious problems with colleagues. This affects the workplace atmosphere and also chances of heading very vital jobs in an organisation where teamwork is very important. It can lead to stagnation after a meteoric rise. Sometimes people face continuous opposition to their ideas in their organisation. This can lead to dissatisfaction in job even though the job may be financially very good.

With the advent of modern technology, many new careers have come up. People are switching jobs frequently. Engineers are into marketing of soaps and detergents. People face a lot of apprehension when they want to switch from one stream to another. Sometimes problem comes up after the switch has been made by a person. Astrology can help natives make better choices out of a host of options. The ill effects of frequently changing jobs can be handled by astrological prescription of gemstones. Many times the opposition to ideas can be countered by prescribing gemstones.

How Gemstones Help Profession:

The primary thing in this analysis is whether the profession a native is pursuing is conducive to indications in the horoscope. There are certain clear indications about the profession, which will be pursued by the native in the horoscope. But there are innumerable areas within a profession, where a particular temperament is required to succeed. The horoscope indicates a personality, which may not suit that kind of job, which the native is pursuing. The basic career remaining the same, the person still has scope to switch a job or switch to some other area of the same career. The use of gemstones can help the native in channelising his energies in a particular manner to achieve better results. Sometimes gems are used for providing healing to the native, so that his performance curve remains high. The temperament of the native can be given a shape for the better by the use of gemstones. But this has to be done after proper assessment of the horoscope of the person.

There are so many things, which have to be taken into consideration while prescribing gems for professions. This task cannot be done without deep astrological analysis of horoscope. Many times gems are prescribed for a very limited period and use. For example when a native is not getting his promotion and it is getting delayed for no specific reason. The relevant planet's strength can be enhanced or a yoga present in the horoscope can be strengthened by using gems. This has proved very helpful in innumerable cases. People going for the interviews are not able to perform well for simple reason of being nervous. This can be rectified by using gems temporarily for certain period of time before the due date of interview to calm nerves. Corporate executives while going for all important presentation to get a business deal worth Millions can get immense benefits from the use of appropriate gems. Various transient conditions experienced by people during certain situations can be controlled very effectively by the use of gemstones.

Even in ancient times, diplomats while visiting a hostile country for negotiations used to wear specific gems to help them in achieving their objectives. All such type of business and official conduct can be affected by the use of dynamic prescription of gems depending upon the effect desired and the prevailing dasa and transits and the horary charts used in such situations. But then, as has been stressed earlier, this dynamic usage of gems is possible only when a professional and proficient advice is constantly available to the native.

The modern day politics world over is full of examples where astrologers are consulted for various things. In ancient times the kings used to employ a team of astrologers for their advice on all-important matters. Many Presidents, Prime Ministers and innumerable politicians have been using the services of astrologers and clairvoyants for advice and guidance. Many have been known to use gems for success in their professions.

In the case of normal people, the change of job and connected problems like lack of job satisfaction, relationships with colleagues and superiors are equally important areas of concern. Many people land up in an area of career which conforms to their qualification but they do not have temperament for that activity. They can get help from gemstones to enhance that required trait for success and satisfaction in their job. Sometimes, they are better if they change their area of activity within the same career. Gemstones can be prescribed to strengthen that trait which is present in horoscope. If the area of activity is also changed towards that indicated by horoscope, then remarkable results can be experienced, as the Gemstones will be even more effective in such cases.

We will discuss the planetary configurations for various professions and the kind of gemstones, which can help that type of professions. Although the prescriptions have to be done on a case-to-case basis, but some general prescriptions can be made safely also.

JUDGES AND LAWYERS

In astrology, Jupiter is the planet, which rules law. Since both lawyers and judges practice law, it is very important planet in their horoscopes. Both the signs owned by Jupiter i.e. Sagittarius and Pisces are also important. The sixth house rules court cases and the ninth house rules law itself. All airy signs are also important especially Libra. If these houses and their lords are strong and connected with tenth house, then the native practices law. Similar combinations if existing in the Dasamsa chart, then the career will be connected with the law. If these combinations have connection with Sun or Leo, then the person gets connected with government and he can be a judge or a government lawyer. The presence of other Rajyogas and their fructification timing can be used to predict the status of a judge and his elevation to higher courts.

Many times in the birth chart these things are not manifest very clearly. In such cases the use of Dasamsa chart and Navamsa chart should be used freely in combination with birth chart. The chalit chart should invariably be constructed to know if any planet is shifting to a different house.

The most important planet for these professions is Jupiter. The astrologer can prescribe Yellow sapphire in most of the cases. But in many cases, the person requires help in some other areas. A judge may need it to get his promotion happen in time. A lawyer requires success in some case. The elevation of a judge may be hanging fire. In all these cases, individual analysis can lead the astrologer to decide on a particular stone to be prescribed. Even dynamic prescription can work wonders in the case of lawyers depending upon the dasa running at a particular time.

POLICE AND MILITARY

Mars is the planet for these professions and the signs ruled by it i.e. Aries and Scorpio would have to be prominent. The third house is house of valour and the sixth house rules wars. These two houses and their lords should be prominent. All the fiery signs are also important.

These planets and signs if connected with tenth lord or prominent in Dasamsa chart, give an indication of these professions. Prominent association of Ketu in tenth house also indicates profession to be of defence department.

In such cases, Red coral is the stone to be prescribed. But due care should be taken that this stone does not get associated in any way with the marak planets of the horoscope as in such cases, it will give energy and fire to the native to fight but can lead to death also. Depending upon other combinations and dasa operating, native can be prescribed other stones for highlighting other good yogas present in horoscope to help the career of the native.

ENGINEERS

If in a horoscope of native the influence of Rahu and Ketu is prominent, the native can be engineer. Mars is the planet of tools and Saturn indicates use of tools. Venus affects the refinement in the use of tools. If these are prominent, then the person is sure to become engineer. These things should be prominent in the Dasamsa chart as well to give a conclusive answer. The signs owned by these planets are also important.

Many times the person goes through the engineering education and then does not work as an engineer. This is due to various dasa operating. The Saturn if not prominent, the person may not work as an engineer as he will not be using tools. These combinations are present in the horoscope of many IAS officers who studied as engineers.

The best stone for the engineers are dependent upon the prominence of a particular planet due to which he becomes engineer. Red coral works very well for mechanical engineers in their work. Diamond can help these people in using the upcoming technology with finesse. This can help people in the field of Information technology, Software development as these are fast changing fields. If Saturn is strengthened with Blue sapphire, then it can be of immense help in improvements in tools and equipments. But it depends upon case to case and cannot be generalized. If there is strong connection with Sun or Leo with tenth house, then the person will work for government

MEDICAL PROFESSION

Ketu is the most prominent planet in the horoscopes of the doctors. In addition Sun, Mars and Jupiter should also be strong. Sun being the life-giving planet, must be strong to be a good doctor. Jupiter is the greatest healer and should be prominent. Sign of Scorpio rules drugs, medicines etc. Hence, its lord should be strong as well. Pisces governs doctors as well. In the case of doctors, the sixth house or its lord should be connected with the 10th house. If Mars or Ketu are very strongly connected with the tenth house and its lord, it makes the native a surgeon.

Cats eye is the stone for the doctors combined with yellow sapphire for Jupiter being a healer. For surgeons Venus should be strengthened with Diamond as it gives them finesse of using very fine tools. Other combinations can be used depending upon the requirements and the dasa operating for the native.

FINANCE PROFESSIONALS

Mercury is the ruler of accounts. Jupiter is the ruler of Law. 2nd House and sign Taurus are connected with finance. If these factors are prominent and connected with tenth house, then the person goes into the finance field. Connection with Jupiter results in a person being Chartered accountant. Other combinations and prominent planets can lead to a person becoming finance professional of various types like banker, stock broker, financial controller etc. Stock analyst has very good fifth house and its lord, as he is required to predict the future of stock market. Strong 5th house and its lord give the person ability to predict future events. This house also rules intuition.

The best stone for the financial professionals is Emerald. But depending upon the other factors in horoscope, the astrologer can prescribe other stones also. Yellow sapphire with emerald works very well for Chartered accountants and income tax consultants. It has been observed that dynamic prescription works with such people very well as there are day to day changes in many of the finance professions like stock analyst. The fifth house and its lord should be strengthened by appropriate gems for such persons and dynamic prescription on the basis of transit and dasa-antardasa should be beneficial for them.

We discuss the case of a Bank executive. The person whose chart is below was born in Nainital (details are being withheld as per request of the native). The chart is given below.

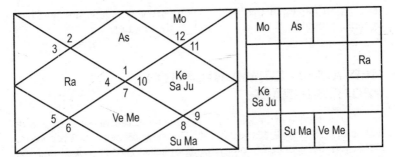

Chart of Bank Executive.

This native was posted out of his home state to a far-flung place and he had lot of problems in his career. Many investigations started and he was not promoted also at the due date. This happened when his Moon period started and Moon being in 12th house had to give him transfer to a far away place. Moon Rahu period gave him lot of troubles in his career. This just retarded his progress in career. But the planetary combinations do not show too much bad results. That is what happened. He was asked to wear a Pearl and a Blue Sapphire later.

His case for promotion was processed and simultaneously all inquiries finished favourably for him. He was transferred to his home state as well and was given the promotion as well after some time. His antardasa periods also changed but the powerful effects of Gemstones helped him get out of inquiries even during Rahu period. This case tells us the power of Gemstones in helping the native.

ARTISTS AND PERFORMERS

The main planet for fine arts, Music and Dancing is Venus. The association of Venus with Moon, Mercury, and Jupiter gives artistic talents. The houses owned by Jupiter in horoscope should be prominent. Third house and Mercury should also be prominent. A strong fifth house and its lord show creative abilities. In case of singers, the 2nd house and its lord, which rules speech, should be strong. Any mix of these combinations connected with tenth house can lead to arts and performing arts as profession.

Diamond suits most of the artists and performers. Only in those cases where it is marak planet, it should not be used. In other cases, it is safe as Venus is a natural benefic planet. A case-to-case analysis is very important, as in this field numerous combinations are possible. Dynamic prescription works very well in these cases.

MEDIA AND COMMUNICATION PROFESSIONALS:

This category of people must have communication skills of a very high order. This includes journalists, TV newsreaders, and reporters. Mercury is the planet of communication skills. The 2nd house and the lord of 2nd house have effect on the speech of a native. In case of writers and writing professionals, 3rd house becomes important as well as it rules over writing abilities.

In most cases, Emerald can be used safely. Mercury is a natural benefic planet, it suits most people. It should not however, be used in those natives where Mercury is malefic or lord of malefic houses. Sometimes the yogas present in the horoscope involving 2nd house and Mercury need enhancement to give the professional side of the native a boost. But while enhancing these yogas, conflict of gemstones should be given due attention.

In those cases where Emerald cannot be prescribed, the gemstones for other planets influencing the communication abilities are prescribed. It must be remembered that assessment of a horoscope is a complex process. Gemstones should be used after weighing both positive and negative influences in a chart on case-to-case basis.

EDUCATIONISTS:

In this category of profession teachers, professors and such people who are involved in academic development are included. In all such cases, one can find that Mercury is generally placed favourably being planet of intellect. It usually is in close conjunction with Sun as well. In many such cases, it is found that Jupiter also becomes prominent in the chart. Jupiter is karaka for teachers and preceptors.

In these cases, gemstones prescribed for planets posited in 5th house can help these natives. If Jupiter or Saturn is prominent in chart then their gemstones can also be prescribed provided they do not own evil houses. In cases where close Budhaditya yoga is present, combination stone should be used to enhance this yoga.

Chapter 9

Marriage, Love Life and Gemstones

Introduction:

Marriage is a major milestone in the life of man or a woman. After marriage, a lot of changes happen due to the commitment of living with another person itself. Vedic philosophy accords great importance to the institution of marriage. Hindus, consequently, have a deep and sacred respect for this social obligation. This aspect makes them go for matching of horoscopes before marriage. Since the marriage has to be in time, they go for arranged marriages as well. This arranged marriage is not very popular concept in West. Since arranged marriages are like treading the unknown, people are apprehensive about then. They want to know the outcome of marriage and the future of married life. Vedic system has astrology as its integral part, which can guide a person for marriage with a particular person. There are well-established ancient tenets of horoscope matching of prospective persons intending to marry in Vedic astrology. These tenets cover all aspects of the married life and guide the native about marriage.

But nowadays, just like western cultures, even in India marriages do not necessarily happen in old fashion arranged manner. Young couples are dating each other and end up marrying without the matching of horoscopes. These days more women are working out of their homes. This leads to more marriages happening without matching of horoscopes. The result is that many such marriages go through lot of turmoil. Sometimes the problems are lopsided as the horoscope of one person may have combinations for marital felicity but the other partner may not have. Thus, the marriage may look fine but one partner suffers. Generally, such problems can be helped by prescribing right type of gemstones to one or both the partners.

Apart from some of the love marriages having problems, even arranged marriages encounter similar problems. These marriages hit a rough patch even after matching of horoscope. These problems can be due to a host of factors. Even during matching of horoscopes some of the factors do not match but the overall match is good and marriage happens. But that factor does erupt sometimes in the life and creates problems in married life. We have to be clear that a perfect match is not possible in this world. A compromise has to be there to go for a marriage. Sometimes, the dasa and antardasa period of a native can have adverse effect on the married life. Even transits of slow moving planets can affect one of the partners and lead to some marital discord. These problems can be handled very effectively by prescribing the right gemstones to one or the both partners.

Another type of relationship of present times is live-in relation. Partners due to various factors do not get married but continue to live together. They also want stability in this relationship and cordiality as well. Many times such couples also seek help for maintaining the relationship. Gemstones can help such people as well.

Another problem which many people face is the problem of delayed marriages. Most of the times we find parents of natives are worried as their children do not get married in time. This happens more in the case of girls. Many times even social pressures mount in these cases. This problem is not confined to India, but even in western countries it is there. If a girl is not dating a boy in her young age, then it is considered that something is wrong somewhere. Gemstones can help people in getting over effects of planets which delay and retard marital prospects.

Marriage karakas:

In order to understand the problems in marriages and love life of people astrologically, we should first know the influences in a horoscope, which affect these areas of life.

Venus is a planet, which is karaka for marriage and love. In the case of females, Jupiter also influences marriage. The 7th house of a horoscope and the lord of the 7th house are also karakas for love, partnerships and marriage. Influence of Mars is high as far as passion, sex life and libido is concerned. In case of Males, Venus is the karaka for semen and potency. The 12th house of the horoscope has bed pleasures under its domain. Mercury being an eunuch planet can cause impotency in males. Thus, its effect must be considered closely.

Saturn being a slow malefic planet can lead to retarding influence on marriage while afflicting 7th house. Mars is a malefic in some positions as far as married life is concerned. It can delay marriages and causes a major dosha in a chart.

Thus, it can be seen that the love life and marriages pivot around a number of factors in a horoscope. The whole scenario is quite complex and can cause problems to people. If the Dasa and antardasa of a malefic planet is running, then such problems get compounded. But if the chart is interpreted correctly, then majority of the problems can be solved to a large extent by use of appropriate Gemstones.

Role of Mars in Marriage:

Mars is a very important planet as far as love life and marriages are concerned. Mars is karaka for passion in a person. Along with Venus in a chart, it also controls libido in a person. But Mars can wreak havoc also in these matters in certain positions in a chart.

Mars when posited in 1st, 2nd, 4th, 7th and 8th or 12th house of a horoscope causes Manglik dosha. Mars aspects the 4th house, 7th and 8th house from its position. It is a fiery planet and a natural malefic as well. Thus its aspects can cause problems. The aspects of Mars in the above stated positions affect the 7th house, 4th house of family life and 8th house of longevity in some way or the other. But Mars is not always malefic even in these positions. There are certain exceptions to the above positions as well. If mars is well disposed and aspected by benefics or placed in own house etc., it does not cause Manglik dosha. A complete discussion on this topic is beyond the scope of the book. But a table below gives whether Manglik dosha exists or not as per the ascendant in the chart.

Gemstones help in mitigating the malefic effects of the Manglik dosha. Actually, horoscope matching is must when the Manglik dosha exists. But when the marriage has happened already and problems crop up, then gemstones can be used for reducing the malefic effect of this dosha. In many cases this dosha delays marriages. In such cases native can be asked to wear Red coral to propitiate the planet Mars. Red coral is the stone for Mars and has proved effective in many cases. The only thing is that care should be taken that Mars has no ownership of marak houses. In such cases the ill effects can also increase. Thus a proper assessment of chart has to be done to arrive at appropriate gemstone.

Chart Showing **Manglik Dosha** For All Asendent

House	Aries	Taurus	Gemini	Cancer	Leo	Virgo	Libra	Scorpio	Sagittarius	Capricorn	Aquarius	Pisces
	1	2	3	4	5	6	7	8	9	10	11	12
1st	N	Y	Y	N	N	Y	Y	N	Y	N	Y	Y
2nd	Y	N	N	N	N	Y	N	Y	N	Y	Y	N
4th	N	N	Y	N	N	Y	N	N	Y	N	N	Y
7th	N	N	Y	N	N	Y	N	N	Y	N	N	Y
8th	N	N	N	Y	N	N	N	Y	N	N	N	N
12th	N	N	N	N	N	N	Y	N	N	Y	N	Y

Y = "Yes";   **N = "No"**

We will discuss a case of a Lady born on 29th August 1979 at 2:35 AM in New Delhi. Her chart is given below. One can easily see that in her case Mars is in 1st house and does not fall within exceptions and causes Manglik dosha. She was not getting married and the parents were worried. She also wanted to marry a colleague. This was causing some delay. Her father approached and she was prescribed Yellow Topaz for Jupiter as it is 7th house lord. This ultimately led to a situation where the family agreed for the marriage with the boy of her choice and it was solemnized with in 6 months in January 2004. Though benefic effects of Jupiter have helped her but it is still foreseen that she will have some marital problems due to Mars in 1st house aspecting 4th, 7th and 8th house. The father of the girl was made aware of this fact before marriage as well.

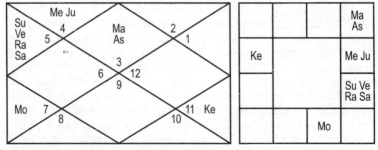

Chart of lady born on 29/08/1979 at 2:35 hrs at New Delhi.

We have another case of a lady born on 7 Sept. 1979 at 20:45 hrs at Bombay. The birth chart is given below. The lady has Mars in her 4th house and it forms a Manglik dosha in her chart, as it is not in any exception also. Her parents approached the author to discuss her marriage not happening despite proposals coming. The Mars in 4th house delays marriage here. Her Darakaraka is Jupiter and is placed in 6th house. Actually her 5 planets are in 6th house, creating troubles for her. Moon in 7th house of Navamsa chart is a saving grace. She has been advised Red coral in gold ring for propitiating Mars along with other remedies. The problem was any proposal coming would be rejected by someone or the other in the family. But after she wore the ring, her parents have approached for match making with one of the boys who meets approval of all in the family. The marriage may fructify in near future.

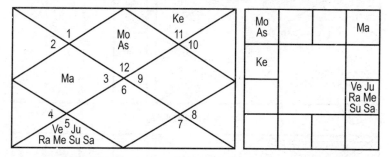

Chart of Lady born 07/09/1979 at 20:45 hrs at Bombay.

Enhancing Love life by Gemstones:

In today's times the marriages are happening when people get well settled in life. Ancient people were entering into marriages as and when the puberty age was reached. The age for marriages has increased to 28-30 years in general. This leads to people entering into relationships with opposite sex. Dating has increased and courtships last for years together. Thus, it has opened up problems of couples in their love life. In majority of the cases, if we examine the birth charts of both the partners, we find no major problem. But still some niggling things souring the relationships can be seen. In most of the cases, it is the dasa/antardasa and the unfavourable transits especially of slow moving planets.

In such cases, the influence of malefic planets on 7th house are studied closely and the affliction to 7th house lord is also studied. Venus and its strength, position and afflictions for both partners are studied.

Thus, a holistic picture is created astrologically for the couple and both or one of them is prescribed the appropriate gemstone. The experience tells us that gemstones can help restore the balance in conjugal relationships.

We will discuss the case of a couple here. Both are working for the Government of India. They have two children. All things seem fine in their marital life. But when they interacted with the author, some problems of adjustment were noticed. They sought some remedy for these personal problems. Their charts are given below.

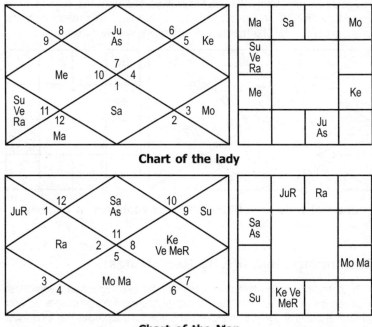

Chart of the lady

Chart of the Man

The Moon dasa of the Man was running and in his birth chart one can see that Moon is conjunct Mars in 7th house. This is aspected by Saturn from 1st house. The problem was with their sex life. It was found during interaction with the man that he was not satisfied with his sex life. It can be seen that Moon dasa and Moon conjunct Mars will definitely affect his mind with extra passion and influence of Saturn on this will give him thinking for some fancy sexual activities. In the case of Lady, Jupiter dasa was running and Jupiter gives you natural pious ness and traditional way of thinking. Thus the passion of man was not at all supported by his wife in this period. Moreover, Saturn debilitated is with Mars in the 7th house of bhava chart. This retards her passion for sex in life. Jupiter aspects this combination which does not allow her to indulge in fancy sex which her husband is interested in. This mismatch was the root cause of problem in their life.

The lady was advised to wear a Red coral in gold ring till the Jupiter period lasts to give boost to her passionate side of life. The man was advised to wear a Pearl in silver ring to control the thought process. Moreover, Moon being Darakaraka, Pearl will help in understanding the viewpoint of his wife properly without being blind about his needs. After around 4 months, both visited the author and without enquiring they told that they were satisfied with the stability they achieved in their personal relationship.

The case study shows that time bound dynamic prescription can help people in a lean phase of their love life. But all this works on a case-to-case basis, as every person is unique with unique planetary combinations. A general prescription does not work. The unique nature of every chart and various divisional charts has to be given due importance while deciding about the Gemstone.

Chapter 10

Gems and Diseases

Introduction:

Gemstones have healing powers also. This fact was known to ancients. All ancient systems had some form or the other of using the gemstones for healing purpose. Be it Indian, Chinese or Tibetan, all had faith in the curative power of Gemstones. They always used these gemstones along with other systems of indigenous medicines.

It is a well-known fact that Sun is the life giver for all living beings on earth. It is this energy, which sustains all activity for living beings. All living beings have a distinct energy balance in their physiology. The Sun energy is in the form of rays and this light energy is composed of seven colours in addition to the infrared and ultraviolet part of this energy. The human physiology also has a peculiar predominance of a particular energy frequency and it ultimately decides the psychological and biological make up of that person. A person having balance of energy in his body is healthy. But once this balance is disturbed, then diseases attack the body. The purpose of any healing system is to restore this energy balance. In many systems, it is done by strengthening particular organs to come back to normalcy and restore balance. In some systems, it is done by using Sun energy itself. This is Gemstone healing.

Gemstones have a typical colour in them and when Sun energy is passed through them then only a particular frequency corresponding to that stone becomes available. This energy is used for restoring balance of energy in the body. Various diseases affect the body differently and hence different types of energy are required for restoring the energy balance. Thus, an experienced diagnosis has to be made to assess as to which gemstone will be best suited for a particular disease.

Astrology also has a vital link in this system. Astrology will indicate which planet has a potential to cause diseases and is in a weak position. This also helps in diagnosing the deficiency. Since that planet has a gemstone associated with it, it becomes very easy to identify the type of gemstone or the type of combination of gemstones required for medical use.

It is also a fact that the damage to organs in the body cannot be restored. Even the highly researched and advanced allopathic system of medicine has not achieved this. The damaged lungs are removed. Gall bladder removal with gallstones has become a routine surgery. Amputations are also carried out. Thus, restoring loss of organ is not possible. Gemstones also cannot do this. But what they achieve is that the deficient energy is made available through gemstone and hence creates conducive energy balance and relief is observed. People whose gall bladder is removed have to live with many precautions. But gemstones can help such people in having an energy balance of the body. Gemstones are used with other systems of medication. They help in feeling better as the energy balance is what they maintain and recovery with medicines of any system is much faster.

This topic is worth a full treatise and in a book on gemstones only limited level of discussion can take place. We have discussed the medical effects of gemstones of various types at appropriate places. Here we will discuss certain diseases with astrological factors and then gemstones used for their treatment. Exhaustive discussion on diseases is beyond the scope of such a book.

1. ASTHMA:

Ashthma is a disease, which affects the lungs of an individual. The bronchial tubes are narrowed due to spasms and an excess of mucous is secreted which makes breathing very difficult for the patient. The patient gets attacks of this and during attacks medical attention has to be sought. Many drugs are used to keep the bronchial tubes dilated to prevent such attacks.

Astrologically Leo sign has lot to do with afflictions of the lungs. Jupiter rules over lungs in astrology. Saturn governs the breathing. Saturn is by nature an obstructive planet. When Saturn afflicts Leo or Jupiter is in Leo and afflicted, then person is prone to asthma. There can be other influences in a horoscope afflicting the 4th house. Leo getting afflicted in the chart and Jupiter weakening also leads to propensity of a native for asthma.

Gemstones are used for asthma very effectively. The gem for the 4th house lord can be used to help if the same planet does not own a marak house as well. Similarly, for breathing difficulty Blue Sapphire can also be combined to get relief but caution and due assessment has to be done. For Jupiter Yellow Sapphire can give very good results along with other stones as discussed above.

2. DIABETES:

Diabetes is a chronic disease. But then it is not a painful disease and is also not a contagious one. The main symptoms are excessive urination and sugar in it, excessive thirst. Here basically the disease is caused by the fact that sugar management system of the body does not work or works inefficiently. The insulin levels are a determinant of the efficiency of the system. Insulin is produced by Pancreas. Due to malfunctioning, body is not able to use up the sugar, starches etc. and sugars accumulate in blood stream and Kidneys react to immediately pass these off in urine. Due to this thirst increases and urination also increases. Here patients suffer loss of weight despite normal diet and sometimes fatigue is also a symptom. Obesity is one problem, which can trigger this disease, and obese people have to be very careful.

Jupiter is the planet, which governs the organs liver as well as pancreas. This is a disease, which is due to Jupiter as this is the planet which controls production of bile and which helps digestion of sugars and starches. When Jupiter is afflicted in Libra or Scorpio, or Jupiter is debilitated or in Aquarius and is placed in a Dusthana, then this disease can affect that native.

Yellow Sapphire can give many benefits to such patients and even White coral combined with Yellow Sapphire helps. White coral helps if the Venus is also afflicted in the horoscope.

3. INSOMNIA:

Sleeplessness over a long period of time is insomnia. This is a modern day disease in the sense that fast pace of life and longer hours of working have led to people working odd hours. In ancient times, people never worked after sunset, as they could not see. Electricity has changed it such a way that now 24 hours working is there. People work in shifts and normal patterns of sleep get disturbed and affliction starts and ends up as insomnia.

This being a lifestyle disorder affects people having moon and Mercury in their horoscope in a weak placement. Excessive fatigue, smoking, alcoholism, coffee and tea in excess are all factors for its aggravation.

The basic cure for this disorder is relaxation of mind and body. Control of anxieties and worries. Change in lifestyle. But in chronic cases all this takes a lot of time to happen and many times planetary configuration is not conducive for a person to do all this on its own. Since this is not an organ related disease, hence gemstones can help very effectively.

The main concerned planets are the Mercury, Moon and Jupiter. Mercury lords over the brain nerve centres. These nerves control our emotions, anger and such activities. This further controls the communication system of the body. Thus, nerves actually play a vital role in insomnia. Thus, Moon which controls mind and thoughts and Mercury, which controls the nerves, need to be in proper balance to get rid of insomnia.

Thus Emerald and Pearl or Moonstone is very helpful in curing insomnia. Sometimes Yellow Sapphire is also used in those cases where the Jupiter has influence on any of these planets.

4. IMPOTENCY:

This is a condition in which a male native suffers from erectile dysfunction so that he cannot have an sexual intercourse. It can happen due to nervous injuries or disorders, alcoholism etc.

Scorpio sign of the zodiac governs the private parts. Mars is the ruler of this sign. Thus, Mars causes all such problems. Malefics in the 7th or 8th house can cause such troubles. Mercury governs the nerves and Mercury in 8th or 12th house also causes this disease.

The gems Red Coral and Yellow Sapphire can give relief in such disorders. But if the affliction is due to presence of Mercury in a weak position in 7th house, impotency can result. Mercury is an impotent planet. Emerald can be used in such cases.

5. MENTAL ILLNESSES:

Most of the mental illnesses are temporary problems of memory and power to concentrate. There is no organic degeneration of brain involved here. It also does not involve any mental deficiency. It is basically losing control over one's mental faculty. The causes for mental illnesses can be varied. It can be due to some brain injury, anxiety, damage to some nerve of brain, tumour of brain, blood clotting in brain, drug addiction etc. Sometimes common people describe such mental illness as nervous breakdown. This can disorient a person from normal activity. Loss of memory or memory lapses is a part of such illnesses. Mental illnesses can be like mania, hysteria, neurasthenia and insanity. Insanity is a condition where person forgets the difference between right and wrong.

Moon, Mercury and Saturn are three planets, which are involved here. Moon is representative of mind and thought processes. Mercury rules over the nervous system. Saturn is a malefic and it retards and afflicts both these planets badly. 3rd and 9th houses are representative of mental things. Gemini, Virgo and Aquarius are the three signs, which are involved and rule over mind and mental structure. Any affliction to these signs by malefics can give rise to mental disturbances. Rahu or Saturn with Moon is enough to cause such ailments. When Mars afflicts Sun or Mercury in Gemini or Virgo, the native can suffer from lunacy.

These conditions and afflictions are controlled by using Emerald, Moonstone and Yellow Sapphire. In cases involving Mars, Red Coral may be required in addition to other stones.

6. MENSTRUAL TROUBLES:

Menstruation is a normal physiological process in females. When it does not follow the cyclic order, then it becomes a disease. The fertile years of a woman have this cycle going on every month. A missed period is an indication of pregnancy. Otherwise, it is trouble.

The planets, which are involved in this process, are Moon, Mars, Venus and Saturn. The key planet is Moon, which governs the actual flow and duration of the blood. Mars governs the blood and the breakage of uterine tissues. Mars is also responsible for starting the flow by causing breakage of uterine tissue. The flow is under the domain of Moon. Moon also governs over impregnation, conception etc. Hence, if Moon is afflicted in birth chart, such troubles can arise. Affliction to Moon in

Scorpio by mars causes pain and profuse bleeding. If Mars, Moon and Venus are in the 8th house, the native suffers from heavy bleeding. If Saturn afflicts Venus in 8th house, then scanty discharge results with pain.

Mars in 7th or 8th house at birth time in a female causes serious troubles in urinary tract and reproductive system. It causes heavy bleeding and even indicates surgeries .Any affliction to Moon or Mars in 7th or 8th house will give rise to menstrual disorders.

The main Gemstone for these disorders is White Pearl. It helps in regulating the duration of flow. Red coral should be used when blood related disorder is also there in case of a native like excessive bleeding.

7. ARTHRITIS:

Arthritis is also called rheumatism in medical terminology. It is basically inflammatory disease of the joints of knees and other joints as well. This can degenerate and even leads to disability. This is a chronic disease even affecting a person for years and many times leads to deformities. It can appear suddenly but generally the disease emerges slowly. Degenerative type or Arthritis occurs in old age. The disease becomes painful at times and especially in winter season. Anxiety and stress also contribute to this disease.

Astrologically, the planets Sun, Moon and Mars in Ascendant of a birth chart may cause Arthritis and similar condition like gout. Capricorn governs our knees and joints. Saturn being ruler also governs joints of lower extremities. Mars in 10th house can also cause arthritis. Mars and Saturn in Sagittarius can give this rheumatism and arthritis. Saturn in Lagna and Mars in 9th house can cause arthritis. Mars in Capricorn gives inflammation of Knee joint and arthritis.

The main planet here is Saturn and Mars. Depending upon involvement of other planets, Red Coral and Lapis Lazuli stones give very good relief results in arthritis. Sometimes Blue Sapphire can be used for Lapis Lazuli. If Jupiter is involved, then Yellow Sapphire can be used. The exact combination can be decided on case-to-case basis.

8. HYPERTENSION:

Hypertension is the name of a disease, which involves high blood pressure. It is a disease connected with heart as heart actually pumps blood in body. High pressure on blood vessels means hypertension. Blood pressure normally increases with age and body weight. Thus, people with obesity can have this disease. Hypertension in younger age is even dangerous as then it connects with lifestyle disorders. Sedentary life actually acts as a boost to hypertension.

Astrologically, hypertension has many planets associated with it. The fourth house has rule over heart and breasts. Moon rules heart. Leo sign deals with matters of heart. Malefics in Leo can cause heart trouble. Three planets in Leo or Aquarius may give rise to hypertension. Medically, it is incurable and modern medicine can only manage it. In such disorders, gemstones are very effective.

Yellow Sapphire and Blue Sapphire have been used for such cases. Sometimes Emerald is also used. In acute cases with afflictions of heart, White pearl is also used.

9. GASTRO INTESTINAL DISORDERS:

Diarrhoea is one of the most common disease. In tropical areas, during summer season, this is a very common affliction. The main symptom is frequent and loose evacuation by the bowels. There are numerous reasons for this disease. Other afflictions of the Gastrointestinal tract are Irritable Bowel syndrome where the bowels reject the food and get irritated very frequently. Dysentery, gastric ulcers are also other disorders.

Astrologically, Cancer and Virgo signs and the 4th and 6th houses rule over stomach and digestive organs. Generally, malefics in transits afflicting them can cause various gastrointestinal disorders depending upon the severity of such affliction. Sun in Cancer or Virgo weakens the digestive organs and can cause constipation. Moon in Virgo if afflicted causes gastric ulcers and derangement of bowels. Ketu in Virgo gives gastric ulcers and Rahu in Cancer or Virgo can cause cancer of the stomach.

Gemstones can be used as permanent remedy for such problems. Emerald and Yellow sapphire are effective in lifestyle type of disorders of Gastrointestinal tract. But in case of ulcers and serious afflictions, specific gem depending upon the afflicting planet and its position in birth chart will help.

10. EYE PROBLEMS:

There are various types of eye troubles. Myopia, farsightedness, near sightedness, conjunctivitis, colour blindness and night blindness. Astrologically Sun is said to govern the right eye and Moon left eye. Malefic planets in the 6th, 8th or 12th house from lagna have power to afflict eyesights and can even cause blindness. Sun afflicting the 2nd and 12th houses can lead to eye disorder. Lord of 2nd and 12th houses occupying dusthanas like 6th, 8th or 12th houses causes various eye diseases. Saturn and Mars conjunct in 2nd or 12th house can cause blindness. Venus Saturn occupying Leo sign can give serious eye troubles. Sun Moon conjunction in 12th and afflicted can cause various eye troubles. Affliction of Sun by Ketu in 2nd or 12th house will cause cataract.

Thus, we see that 2nd house, 12th house and Sun Moon are the key planets in the case of eye diseases. Thus gemstones can be prescribed for these diseases in keeping with the type of affliction and the planets involved. The diseases can be tackled by these gemstones but eye defects are difficult to be cured. But gemstones help the native in getting healed if the treatment or surgery is being carried out for the defects.

11. CIRRHOSIS OF THE LIVER:

Liver as we know is a detoxifier in the body and is largest gland of the body. It produces bile and this helps in digestion of the food. In this disease, the liver hardens. The normal cells are replaced by hard tissue. Water starts accumulating in liver and it increases in size. The reasons are alcoholism, deficiency of vitamin B etc.

Astrologically, 5th house in a horoscope governs our stomach but 6th sign Virgo rules over liver. Jupiter also governs the liver. When Jupiter or mercury gets afflicted by Saturn or Ketu in Cancer or Virgo, the native can suffer from this disease. Saturn Ketu or Sun Ketu conjunction in 5th house causes this trouble.

Use of Emerald and Yellow Sapphire helps such natives immensely. If used along with the treatment, remarkable recovery is observed.

12. GALLSTONES:

This is a disease in which small stones of lime, bile pigment and cholesterol form in the gall bladder and bile duct. It causes inflammation of the gall bladder and the bile duct also swells. When the bile is blocked, jaundice results and some connected problems also arise. Symptoms can be pain, nausea, vomiting and indigestion.

Saturn in Leo with some more planets in Capricorn at birth may give rise to this trouble. Affliction to Mercury or Virgo in the chart is also a cause for this type of trouble. Red Coral and Emerald help in this disease and sometimes Yellow Sapphire is also used in addition. The regular treatment of the disease should continue. These days the gall bladder itself is removed. Such people always have to take precaution in eating fats and heavy food. These stones can help such patients for life.

13. BACKACHE:

It is one of the most common ailments. The causes are difficult to identify but sometimes the injury can also cause this trouble. Postural problems lead to this disease in many cases. People with sedentary lifestyle and who work sitting for long period of time are prone to this trouble. Straining due to heavy work can lead to backache.

Astrologically, Saturn is the planet causing this trouble. Rahu in conjunction with Saturn also gives this trouble in its period. Libra is the sign, which rules over back, and any affliction here causes backache.

Depending upon the affliction, Blue Sapphire, Hessonite and sometimes Yellow Sapphire also is used for backache.

14. THROAT PROBLEMS:

There are many types of throat troubles like phayringitis, tonsillitis and laryngitis. The normal troubles are pain in the throat, swelling of tonsils, difficulty in swallowing, and loss of voice or hoarseness. The throat can have red colour, pus in it. There may be fever or chills associated also. This trouble if occurring recurrently is chronic

In chronic cases, Sun and Mars cause this in Taurus. 2nd house governs our throat. Any affliction to 2nd house or bad placement of 2nd house lord will cause chronic problem of throat. Use of Red Coral or if 2nd lord is involved, then gemstone for that planet is also used.

15. ANAEMIA:

Anaemia is the deficiency of red blood cells in the body and it is caused by poor diet and Iron deficiency. It can be due to haemorrhage as well and sometimes due to damage to bone marrow.

Sun if afflicted by Saturn can cause this problem. Rahu and Ketu in Taurus, Leo or Aquarius also result in Anaemia. Jupiter getting afflicted by Mars in Leo also leads to Anaemia. Red Coral should be used along with Yellow Sapphire by these natives and very exemplary results have been seen by using these gemstones.

16. LEPROSY:

Leprosy is one of the oldest diseases and finds mention in ancient texts as well. It is still prevalent in many parts of the world. It is not hereditary disease. Rahu is the chief planet causing this disease. Rahu in 3rd, 6th, 12th house makes a native liable for leprosy. Even Ketu in such placements can cause this disease. When the lord of lagna is conjoined with Mars and Mercury in the 4th or 12th house a Kushta Yoga is formed. Jupiter occupying the 6th house along with Saturn and Moon also causes Leprosy.

Use of hessonite and Red coral jointly helps these people in this disease. It can be cured in early stages but once the limbs are lost, they cannot be recovered.

Chapter 11

Gem Therapy

Introduction:

The sun is our prime source of biological energy, which is also called as life force. If we place a healthy plant in dark but provide all nutrients and water, it will die. Biological life is unsustainable without the sun's vital energy. This is referred in India as "Prana", Chinese recognize it as "Chi" and Japanese call it "Ki". If a live human being is kept away from the sun, he is not healthy and there are many examples of it.

Kirlian photography is one technique, which shows clearly the biological energy in human beings, animals, living fruit, vegetables etc. It can be seen as an Aura extending as lines of force from all these things. If the same Kirlian photograph is taken of processed fruit, it shows little or no biological energy

When a live being dies, our vital force departs and the organic body is invaded by bacteria and it decays. Thus it is the vital force, which actually protects living beings from the bacteria and decay. This is consequently dependent upon Sun energy. We are susceptible to fall ill when our energy reserves become low and various virus and bacteria are likely to invade us. The life force within us is finite; otherwise we would not fall ill or die. We rest and take wholesome foods when we are ill to recover. We actually try and recover the life's vital force. When we are young, we have abundance of biological energy. With increasing age, it reduces and we also change habits to conserve it. In Ayurveda, emphasis is to restore the biological energy balance. Similar other practices like acupuncture, herbal medicines etc. try and achieve this.

Basis of Gem Therapy:

The gem therapy also intervenes to restore this energy or called Chi. Since different gemstones vary in colour, hence, the type of energy they provide varies in quality. Gemstones emit concentrated rays of strong, pure 'chi' energy of a particular quality depending upon the gem. And ultimately this is the sun energy itself but filtered to provide a concentrated form of particular quality.

Ruby for example emits hot, red rays and is used to treat diseases arising out of cold and dampness. Similarly, Emerald emits cold green rays and is used to treat diseases arising out of too much heat. These effects have been scientifically confirmed by monitoring the patient's pulse or using thermometers or blood pressure meters before and after treatment with gems.

The basis behind it remains the use of Sun's vital energy for specific purpose. The white light from the Sun has a broad spectrum, made up of seven bands of frequencies. These colour bands can be seen in a rainbow. Gem stones emit concentrated form of pure colour using white light energy. The light of Sun or similar artificial light can be used to concentrate required colour light to penetrate the skin, and the beneficial effects are carried deeper by blood.

When we stand near a coal fire, invisible, low frequency infrared rays pass through the body. It crates feeling of heat in the body by speeding up electron activity inside the atoms of tissue and bone marrow as the rays pass through. Concentrated rays of gems influence cellular activity in similar fashion at an atomic level. Here gem therapy scores over other drug therapies as it works at atomic level, where drugs cannot reach.

A beam of Ruby laser in hospital is several times hotter than surface of Sun. It vapourises molecules on contact and can cut through almost any substance. Many crystals can transmute energy from one level to another. Lasers are modern examples of power of gemstones.

Science of Natural Healing Frequencies:

All of us know that rocking or cradling a child back and forth encourages sleep. Most mothers know the speed of such rocking. In fact, this rhythm encourages Delta brain waves and helps baby relax and sleep. Similarly certain other massage can introduce various brain frequencies with resulting corresponding moods. The most important frequencies for promoting healing and their related state of consciousness are listed below:

Brain Rhythm	Frequency	Healing	State of Consciousness
Delta	0.01 – 3.2 Hz	Pain	Deep sleep, no external attention
Theta	3.2 – 7.8 Hz	Trauma	Dreaming, Trance, attention, internal, hypnotic
Alpha	7.8 – 14 Hz	Balancing	Released, attention divided internal and external.
Beta	14 – 30 Hz	Invigorating	Attention focused on external affairs
High Beta	25 Hz plus	Do not Use	Anxiety, Panic, Psychosis etc.

It is a scientific fact that the frequency of the brain's electrical activity is directly connected with health. In the case of anxiety and panic, the frequency of the electrical activity of the patient's brain will be in high Beta that is above 25 Hz. These frequencies are reflected in excess adrenalin, muscular tension, and stress. Simply encouraging the patient's brain activity towards Alpha, or 8.5 Hz. will relieve the symptoms. Meditation or controlling one's internal dialogue has the effect of lowering brain frequencies and producing endorphins, which act like morphine to reduce pain and increase pleasure.

Techniques of Gem Therapy:

There are techniques to use this power of gemstones for healing purposes. The details are discussed below.

1.   WEARING GEMSTONES:

One of the most used practices for the use of gems for healing is the use of gems for wearing. The technique is that the gemstones of large size is worn in rings which are open behind the gem so that light passing through it shined on to the skin and passes on the effects through skin to blood and body. But this system is effective when a person can consult a qualified astrologer frequently and on his advice change the stones periodically as well. In this technique, the uses of properties of various gemstones are used for healing purpose. Specific gemstones are assigned to a planet in astrology and have defined healing properties. A qualified astrologer uses the stones, which are beneficial for an individual by taking into account the planetary configuration as well. This becomes very powerful technique in the hands of a qualified astrologer. The gemstones size is important and normal jewellery size is normally ineffective. This technique requires prolong use of the stones for perceptible benefits.

2.   GEM MEDICINES:

Another technique is the use of gems in preparation of medicines. This technique is widely used in Tibet also. Here the gem medicines are prepared by crushing the gems into a fine paste or burning them to ash. Then these are mixed with selected herbs and oils, which are then made into pills, balms and lotions etc. These medical preparations are very effective provided a trained person is handling the patient. This therapy should not be used as self-medication. This therapy remained confined to royals and the rich only, as the gems are expensive and it becomes prohibitively costly to afford the therapy. Moreover, the gems are wasted also.

Another way of preparing gem medicines is without destroying them. In this technique, the gemstones are placed inside a bottle of 95 % ethanol alcohol. Nine bottles are used, each with a different gemstone. Each bottle contains 4 or 5 cut and polished gems. The nine bottles are then placed in a box and the box is stored in a dark place for 3 months. The remedies are made by spraying blank homoeopathic tablets with alcohol from the bottles as required. This kind of medicine is safe. These gem energy medicines have poor shelf life as the energy is dissipated quickly. These are prepared fresh for the patient and used immediately.

3.   ELECTRONIC GEM THERAPY:

This is the most effective technique as it uses the gem energy very effectively. The instruments for this therapy use special low voltage lamps and contain three lenses that focus the light beam. The gems are placed inside the lamp, together with a coloured filter. The Gem lamps are connected to a precision electronic instrument. The instrument's digital monitor displays the intensity and vibration rate. These both are controlled through control knobs. The benefits are derived as the light energy influences the cohesion and vibration rate of cells, organs and glands.

The low voltage, low heat lamps are completely safe to use. The gems themselves never wear out or depreciate in value. Nothing is ingested, so there are no side effects. The effects are immediately felt by the patient and therapist can control the conditions as he carries on with treatment. The instant feedback gives therapist to change gems if required.

Electronic gem therapy can be usefully employed in conjunction with surgery, allopathy, Psychiatry, Physiotherapy etc. The use of electronic gem therapy is discussed for various conditions.

- **CHRONIC PAIN**

When we are sleeping or in a state of trance, we do not experience pain. The frequency of the brain waves is delta for sleep and Theta for trance. Every part of our body is connected to the b rain via the nerves. Nerves carry the electrical signals back and forth between the brain and the body. As we fall asleep, the body experiences slow delta brain waves in the nervous system. Our organs relax, heart rate slows, blood pressure drops, muscles relax and our aches and pains disappear. Usually when we wake, the pains of the previous day are gone, therefore we can conclude that the vibration rates associated with sleep heal the body.

Common sense suggests that applying Delta brain wave frequencies to the site of the injury will reduce pain. In fact, these frequencies are used in Electronic acupuncture and Tens therapy for exactly this purpose. The gem to use in every case of pain is Blue Sapphire. Sapphire emits a calming analgesic energy. It also seems to increase endorphin production. Unlike analgesic and tranquillising drugs, Sapphire does not deplete the patient's energy reserves or cause side effects. On the contrary, the violet energy emitted by Sapphire fills the person with tranquil energy.

In the case of sciatica, violet filtered light and Blue sapphires are pulsed once or twice a second. The site of the injury is located by moving the Gem transducer lamp up and down the patient's spine. The patient will experience a decrease in the pain as the lamp is passed over the injury. It is also helpful to treat the back and sides of the knee joint of the affected leg with a second lamp. The patient will experience profound relief. A single treatment is often sufficient to clear up condition.

Pain associated with new injuries such as surgery, burns, cuts, abrasions, fractures, sprains or bruises should be treated with a mixture of Blue Sapphire and Emerald with green filtered light. The cool rays of Emerald rapidly introduce cold energy into the hot injured cells. The redness will subside and swelling will be reduced and circulation restricted.

- **EMOTIONAL PAIN AND EXHAUSTION**

The pain and emotional shock experienced through bereavement or serious accident is very disruptive to the nervous and endocrine systems. It can ruin appetite and sleep. If the situation persists for any length of time, the patient will become exhausted. When this occurs, infections can take hold causing further biological energy depletion. This situation can be extremely dangerous.

We know from sleep studies that the body heals itself during sleep (Delta brain Frequencies) and the mind heals itself through dreams (Theta brain frequencies). Directing Blue sapphire rays and violet filtered light, at each side of a patient's head induces calming energy directly into the brain hemispheres. The experience is very pleasurable as the energy travels down, via the nerves, to every part of the body. Enhancing the gem and colour treatment with the Theta (dreaming) frequencies will induce a profound state of relaxation. This is accompanied by waves of pleasure, which permeate the whole body. These 'pleasure' waves smooth out emotional disturbances. This therapeutic procedure is named Bliss therapy or Samadhi. Sometimes a small quantity of Diamonds is added to the Sapphire to bring greater clarity and colour to the experience. With eyes closed, many patients report seeing colours. As the treatment progresses, the colours and sometimes visions or images become more vivid.

This is an extremely beneficial therapy, approximately 70% of all patients attending for gem therapy will receive 20 minutes of this treatment regardless of their complaints or what other treatment they may require.

● NERVOUS DISORDERS

The Ayurvedic pharmacopoeia recommends Sapphire for conditions like anxiety, panic, psoriasis, alopecia, migraine and insomnia. Research has already shown that many nervous disorders are accompanied by high Beta brain frequencies.

Most nervous disorders and diseases respond positively to blue Sapphire. Slow, calming frequencies should be used and violet-filtered light. A fast heart and pulse rate can be slowed down with this sort of treatment. Emerald is also important in the treatment of some nervous conditions. Emerald stops diarrhoea and, in a healthy person, may cause temporary constipation. To treat irritable bowel syndrome a mixture of Sapphire and Emerald is used. The Samadhi therapy, mentioned above, is used and in addition the patient's abdomen is treated with a third Gem Lamp containing an Emerald and Sapphire mixture. The slow frequencies of Delta are employed to induce slower and smoother peristalsis and to cool intestinal inflammation. At the same time, the practitioner may calm the pancreas and adrenal glands with Emerald and Sapphire.

● SKIN PROBLEMS

Psoriasis responds well to treatment with Sapphire, violet filtered light and slow relaxing Delta frequencies. One patient developed psoriasis two weeks after she learned that her husband, a long distance lorry driver, had cataracts and was likely to lose his job. She presented for treatment with both hands so painful that she constantly had to wear cotton gloves as protection. Conventional medical treatment had done nothing to alleviate her condition. A single 20-minute treatment began to reverse her condition and new healthy skin was visible after 3 days.

Psoriasis is erratic behaviour of skin cells, which multiply and die too quickly. The skin drops off in flakes leaving sore, red patches. The affected skin can be treated directly with lamps, using Sapphire to calm the Pineal gland, on the crown of the head, is much more effective. This treatment stops itching in a few minutes.

In another case, a 16 year-old girl developed psoriasis after her parents' divorce. She had been prescribed several different steroid creams but the condition continued to spread. She was frightened and upset, and had been told that she may suffer with psoriasis intermittently for the rest of her life. With a single treatment of Sapphire to her head she made a dramatic recovery.

Eczema and dermatitis are treated with Emerald and green-filtered light. Treating the affected skin will reduce redness in minutes. Sapphire should be included if irritation is present. The number of babies suffering from eczema is on the increase. Five years ago the figure was one in ten. Today it is one in seven. Energizing the liver with Emerald and Sapphire has proved effective for babies.

Varicose ulcers are a real problem for old people in cold damp climates, they can result in amputation. The ulcer can penetrate so deeply that the bone becomes infected and this can make patients seriously ill. One 90 year-old lady recovered from a leg ulcer that she had suffered with for 16 years. Specialists had told her that she would have it for the rest of her life. Her ulcer was treated with Ruby and Diamond and the whole leg with a mixture of Carnelian and Diamond. After treatment she reported that her leg was pleasantly tingling with energy. Within 2 months the ulcer had completely disappeared. These Gem mixtures were pulsed at invigorating Beta frequencies. Chilblains have responded to a single 20-minute treatment of Ruby and Diamond.

- **INJURIES**

New injuries such as cuts, burns, bruises, fractures or sprains require a cool analgesic 'Chi' energy, in which case Emerald and Sapphire are used with green light. When pain is present, inducing the sleep frequency of Delta to the injured area can substantially reduce the pain and accelerate healing. Old injuries that are cold or numb require a stimulating energy and frequency to invigorate cells. A Ruby and Diamond mixture with red-filtered light, pulsed at Beta frequencies is used to invigorate the area with hot 'Chi' energy and improve the circulation. Infected injuries should be treated with Yellow Sapphire with blue-filtered light. To prevent the infection spreading, adjacent tissue should be invigorated with Diamond and Carnelian.

- **INFECTIONS AND ALLERGIES**

In autumn and winter the 'Chi' energy falls as the sun weakens and we become more susceptible to infection. Virus infections like the common cold and influenza take hoid by infiltrating the cell's membrane. Once inside, the virus multiplies and spreads to other cells throughout the body.

Conserving and maintaining high levels of 'Chi' is the best way to avoid infections. Carnelian maintains temperature and Diamond invigorates the system, dramatically increasing the patient's energy levels. Influenza and colds respond quickly to a Carnelian and Diamond mixture with orange-filtered light at low Beta frequencies. The sinus, nose, throat and chest should be energized. Carnelian and Diamond can also be used for prevention of infections, they increase cellular coherence and membrane resilience. Asthma and bronchitis also respond well to this treatment. Where an infection involves bacteria, Yellow Sapphire is more effective. This gem is frequently used to clear bacteria infected tissue in injuries.

- ## MUSCULAR AND SKELETAL PROBLEMS

Disabled patients suffering with spastic, athetoid, dystonic and choreiform muscular problems can be helped with Sapphire and violet-filtered light. By pulsing the Gem Lamps at relaxing Delta brain frequencies, the brain signals that cause these conditions can be intercepted. The Gem Lamps are applied at appropriate nerve junctions on the spine or limbs. Acupuncture and acupressure points can also be used. This treatment can relax tense muscles within minutes. Physiotherapists can treat more patients and be more effective by utilizing these techniques. Rheumatism and arthritis respond positively to Diamond and Carnelian energy. In addition, Blue Sapphire is frequently used because it is very effective in dispelling the pain associated with these conditions.

Painful 'clicking' cartilage problems in joints respond to Diamond and Carnelian. One patient had developed this problem as a result of a sports injury to his knee. After ten minutes of this treatment, he said that his 'bad' knee felt better than his 'good' knee. The pain and swelling which accompany sprains, joint injuries or bone fractures should be treated with Emerald and Sapphire mixtures.

Chapter 12

Numerology and Gemstones

NUMBER 1

Western Numerology:

Number 1 is the origin of all numbers and represents the beginning. It stands for the symbol for Sun. Just like Sun is the source of all life, number 1 also represents the origin of all. It also represents creative, individual and things and attitudes, which are positive.

Those who are born under the influence of this number, or any of its connected series numbers, are creative in their own way in their work, they are very individualistic in their approach and very definite about their views. Sometimes these persons can be obstinate in their approach as well. All persons born on 1st, 10th, 19th or 28th of any month fall under this category. Such people are ambitious and do not like to work under constraints. They are natural leaders and rise also in their occupation. They always work to head their organization and once there, they try to maintain a position where they will be at a higher status.

They should try and encash the vibrations on dates which add up to 1, when planning to carry out any important activity. Sunday and Monday are best days for these individuals. Their fortunate colours are shades of yellow and gold to golden brown..

The Gemstones which are beneficial for these people are topaz, Amber, Yellow diamond and all stones in these tones of colour. The system followed is the colour therapy. The orange yellow coloured stones which are associated with number one channelise that part of energy which is much more suitable for the Sun dominated personality and hence augments and benefits the individuals born under number one.

The vibrations due to the colour of these stones are harmonious with the number one and hence a resonance effect continues in their body if such gemstones are used by the number one people. This gives them enhanced benefits.

Vedic Numerology:

In Vedic system of numerology, the number 1 is also representative of planet Sun. But the Gemstone for Sun is Ruby and this stone is prescribed by Vedic practitioners. It does not go by the western thinking of colour-based prescription of Gemstones. Ruby being a transparent gemstone is very powerful and gives number 1 people enhanced benefits from people in power and can make them become themselves powerful if the other indications as per their horoscope are also favourable. In ancient Vedic astrology, Sun Yantra(Numerological totem) is also based on the Number 1 as below.

6	1	8
7	5	3
2	9	4

Sun's Yantra

NUMBER 2

Western Numerology:

The number 2 is the symbol for the planet Moon in numerology. Its attributes and all significations are feminine in nature and the number 2 people are opposite the number 1 people as they are masculine in nature. But the affinity of number 1 and 2 is very high and form a good combination.

These people are romantic, artistic and gentle in nature in keeping with the feminine nature of number 2. They are also very inventive persons. They are, however, very soft in carrying out and implementing their ideas. Since Moon has connection with mind, these people operate at mental level more than at physical level. They need someone to implement their mental ideas in real terms. That is why their combination with number 1 people is very harmonious. Consequently, they are physically not very strong being feminine in nature.

Persons born under 2nd, 11th, 20th or 29th of any month are number 2 people. But then they are having much more pronounced qualities of number 2 if they are born between the 20th June to the 27th July. This period is called the period of Moon.

These people get along very well with number 2 people obviously and even number 1 people, as they are compatible with them and fulfill the void existing inherently in their nature. They can be very Moon like in their nature and wax and wane like Moon. This is a tendency they need to guard against. Moreover, since they operate at mental level, they need to have focus on implementation of ideas. They lack self-confidence as well. They can be melancholic easily and are oversensitive people and should be aware about these negative traits in them.

They get good vibrations from green colour, creams and whites. Dark colours do not suit them. The lucky gemstones for them are Pearls, Moonstone, and pale green stones and Jade. Jade suits them very well.

The colour vibrations that these stones emit are in keeping with the Moon nature and hence they get enhanced benefits out of these stones. They themselves feel good and energetic when they wear such stones only due to the resonance of their inherent vibration with the concentrated similar vibrations from the gemstone.

Vedic Numerology:

The Vedic system also associates number 2 with Moon. The gemstone for Moon is the white pearl and Moonstone. This is same as in the theory of western numerology. Pearl affects the mental aspects of humans. Moon in Vedic astrology represents mind and hence these Gems affect the mental frame of the person wearing them. These gemstones can control their emotional mental energy and help them channelise it into practical realm for success.

The ancient Vedic system has a Yantra for Moon also based on number 2 as the basic number. The Yantra is given below and is also useful for people with number 2.

7	2	9
8	6	4
3	10	5

Moon's Yantra.

NUMBER 3

Western Numerology:

The number 3 is the symbol of Jupiter. It is considered the noble planet and also extremely important planet in Numerology and Astrology. The simple reason is that its association with malefic planet can reduce their malefic results drastically. In numerology, it defines a type of force, which carries through all other numbers after it. This number has a very special relation with every third in the series such as 6 and 9. If added in any way 3, 6, 9 add to ultimately 9. People of 3, 6, 9 have a special affinity between them.

All those born on 3rd, 12th, 21st, or 30th of any month have 3 as their number. But if these people are born between 19th February to March20th-27th or from the 21st November to December 20-27th. This is period of number 3.

Number 3 persons are quite ambitious and want to have a lead in most things. Subordinate positions for them are quite irritating and dissatisfying. They want to control everything in the world. This leads them to try and acquire knowledge of different things. This makes them all rounder also. They love discipline and order in everything. Since they obey orders readily, they expect that their orders should be obeyed as well readily.

All these qualities can take them very high in their life and they rise to higher positions in government, business etc. They are also very good leaders in armed forces. They also rise high in positions of trust and responsibility. This tendency of order and discipline in some cases can become dictator like. This can cause lot of opposition to them and their ideas and the way of implementation of these ideas. They hold lot of pride in themselves and get peeved at many petty things done by other people. It can lead to problems also.

These people should carry out their activities and major plans on 3rd, 12th, 21st, 30th of any month so that they have resonance of good vibrations going in favour. Thursday is very important day being ruled by Jupiter and even Tuesday and Friday are very good. These people are in good harmony with people having 6 or 9 as their number. They can wear mauve, violet, purple colours. They should use these colours also in their rooms and office may be.

The gemstones most suitable for them is the Amethyst. Even other gemstones of violet colour range also suit them very well. Many stones of blue range have shades of violet in them, these can be also worn by them easily. Amethyst works very well for them. Since it is not a precious stone and reasonably priced as well, they must keep one with them to help them.

Vedic Numerology:

However, the Vedic system of astrology and numerology has a different viewpoint here. The planet associated with number 3 is Mars. The Gemstone for Mars is Red Coral and even the ancient Mars Yantra has 3 as its basic number in the Yantra given below. The Vedic system works on a more sound principle as it is not based on colour based prescription of gemstones but is based on the association of planets with the numbers and have the yantras also designed on these basic numbers.

8	3	10
9	7	5
4	11	6

Mars' Yantra

NUMBER 4

Western Numerology:

In numerology, number 4 stands for the symbol of Uranus planet. It is related to Sun and the numbers 1 and 4 are quite related as well. Number 4 persons have a different view for everything. They have an ability to look at things oppositely also. In the process, they can have opposition. They will side with opposite view even though it may not be the right one. They create enemies also due to this attitude. They will have more secret type of enemies than manifest one. They have a remarkable quality to take conflicting stance in anything presented to them. This also leads them to have basic tendency to oppose rules and laws and regulations also. They would take reverse position in community and government matters also. They would walk on a jogging track also in the opposite direction from the mainstream of public.

They can be reformers also. Since they have opposite views, they can bring the other side of coin in perspective. It helps in those issues, which form laws of the government to at least have a look at the other side also before framing the laws. They are also reformist and help all causes of reforms in government, society of personal life as well.

All the persons born on 4th, 13th, 22nd, and 31st of a month are number 4 people. If they are born in the period of Sun and Moon i.e. 21st June to 20-27th July and 21st July to end of August. It is very difficult for these people to make friends. They get attracted to Number 1, 2, 7, 8 people as the element of individuality in these people attracts them.

Due to above qualities, they are not very successful in worldly affairs and even material issues. Accumulation of wealth is not their forte and they are indifferent to it as well. Again if they have money with them, they use it very differently and surprise the normal thinking way of the world. These people are at their best if they carry out their major activities on 4th, 13th, 22nd, 31st of the month. The fortunate days for them are Saturday, Sunday and Monday. If their own number date falls on these days, then it is more fortunate. They can derive the benefits of resonating vibrations then.

Their main drawback is that they are highly strung persons. They get hurt very easily and turn lonely to melancholic. More so, if they are not successful, they are depressed people in life. They do not make large number of friends but once they are friends then they are loyal and most devoted to them. The person who is underdog in life will find such people rallying for them.

Their lucky colours are electric colours or half shades and tones. Electric blue and grays suit them best.

The best gemstone for these people is Blue sapphire in all its shades and it is advisable for them to wear it all the time. Other gemstones of half shades like Lapis Lazuli also works very well for them.

Vedic Numerology:

The Vedic system associates, again differently from western system, planet Mercury with the Number 4. The Gemstone for the persons with number four would be Emerald and not based on the colour-based system of western thinking on Numerology. Even the numerology based Yantra of Vedic system for Mercury has 4 as basic number as below.

9	4	11
10	8	6
5	12	7

Mercury's Yantra

NUMBER 5

Western Numerology:

This number 5 represents Mercury. The number is very versatile and is mercurial in its qualities and characteristics. All those born on 5th, 14th, and 23rd, of any month are number 5 people. Their qualities are more pronounced if they are born in the period of number 5. It is 21st May to June 20-27th and 21st August to Sept 20-27th.

Number 5 people are very affable and friendly. They make friends easily. They get along with practically all types of people. Their best friends are found under the number 5 only. These people are also very highly-strung type. They love excitement. They are very quick in their thoughts and actions and represent Mercury characteristics in Human form. They can be impulsive also and they drift towards all methods of making money easily. They can have a very keen sense of making money due to new ideas and inventions also. They tend to speculate a lot and play in stock market also and they take risks also.

The character and behaviour of number 5 people is elastic. They can recover from any blow in life very easily as if nothing happened. Nothing persists with them. Their character stays the way it is just like Mercury can get shaped in to any form but still retains its characteristics. But if they are good, they remain good. If they are bad, nothing can reform then at all.

These people should carry out their plans on 5th, 14th, 23rd of any month and especially in the period of number 5. Wednesday and Friday are very lucky days for them.

They have a drawback in the sense that they can have nervous breakdowns as they exhaust themselves completely. Under mental tension, they can become irritable and quick tempered. Their lucky colours are all shades of light gray, white and glistening materials. Actually they can wear any colour but glistening shades are good for them. Dark colour do not suit them.

Their lucky stone is Diamond and all glittering things as well. Platinum and Silver jewellery also suits them very much. They should keep wearing Diamonds through their life.

Vedic Numerology:

The Vedic system of numerology associates number 5 with Jupiter. The gemstone for Jupiter is Yellow sapphire and hence, this stone can give benefits to number 5 people. The ancient Numerology based Yantra for Jupiter has the basic number as 5 as below.

10	5	12
11	9	7
6	13	8

Jupiter's Yantra

NUMBER 6

Western Numerology:

This number 6 is the symbolism for the planet Venus. All those persons who are born on 6th, 15th, and 24th of any month are persons under this number. This becomes especially so if they are born under the period of number 6 i.e.20th April to May 20th-27th and from 21st September to October 20th-27th.

These people have something extremely attractive about them and they tend to attract others towards them naturally. This leads to these persons with 6 number getting loved by others more often than not. They are at times worshipped by people who get attracted towards them and are under their influence.

Number 6 people are very deterministic in nature and will do anything to carry out their plans and ideas. They can become unyielding and even obstinate many times. But if they love something deeply, then they can become completely devoted to that person and behave like slaves. These people love art and decorate their homes artistically also. They show Venusian qualities very often like appreciating art and music. If they have money, then they tend to patronize arts and artists also. They love to make everybody happy and entertain their loved ones to make them happy. They hate jealousy and discords of any kind and feel irritated about these things in life.

They are also very deterministic in their causes. If they oppose something, they will oppose it to the hilt. If they become angry, then they will oppose that issue or person till death. These qualities in number 6 people make them ending up having more friends than any other number except number 5. They get along very well with people in the number series of 3, 6 and 9.

The important day for them is Friday, Thursday and Tuesday. These people should carry out their major plan and activities on the dates with 3, 6 and 9 number. Their lucky colours are the shades of blue from light to darkest, all shades of rose pink. Black and dark purple colours do not suit them.

Their gemstone is Turquoise. They should wear this always. They also get lot of benefits by wearing Emeralds. These stones help them calm down in their thinking and the stubborn tendencies are mellowed and help them. Their devotion to love and become slave of the person they love is also halted to an extent by using Turquoise.

Vedic Numerology:

The Vedic system also associates Venus planet with number 6 just like western system. But then the prescription of gem is also based on planet rather than colour based system. Their gemstone is diamond and number 6 people can derive rich benefits by wearing diamond. The Vedic Yantra for Venus is also based on basic number of 6 as shown below.

11	6	13
12	10	8
7	14	9

Venus Yantra

NUMBER 7

Western Numerology:

This number 7 stands for planet Neptune as per numerology and represents all persons born under the 7th, 16th, 25th of a month. They get pronounced qualities of number 7 if they are born in the period of number 7 i.e. between 21st June to July 20th-27th. Neptune is very closely associated with Moon. Neptune also is very highly connected with water also.

Number 2 for the Moon has a very close relation with Number 7. These people have 2 as their secondary number and get along very well with people born under the number 2. Number 7 people are very original and in everything they do, their individuality is visible. They love to travel and changeability is very close to them. They are restless by nature, they will try and move around visiting as many countries as possible. This tendency gives them a penchant for travelogues and they end up getting very wide knowledge about the world as such.

They can turn out very good writers, painters or poets but then they have a typical philosophical touch to everything they do. Since they have originality, they get rich due to original ideas. Though, they care very little about the material things in life. They are inclined to give large donations to charities from their wealth if they have it.

The number 7 have very original and good ideas about business but they lack the full capacity of carrying out these ideas. If they carry out their ideas, they are brilliant and extremely successful people. They are very good as sailors, captains of ships and business, which involves traveling. In matters of religion also they are original. They abhor the age-old ideas in religion and have their own philosophy about it. These people have a natural intuition and gift for occult.

These people should carry out their major activities on dates which are number 7. The best days for them are Sunday and Monday and more so if their number date falls on them. Their lucky colours are all shades of Green, pale shades and dark colours do not suit them.

Their lucky stone is Moonstone and white pearls. If possible, they should wear a moonstone all the time. The vibrations of Moon get channelised and then their inner potential gets activated and they have very great power to come up with ideas. It helps them get control over their lives and not get swayed away in their philosophical outlook.

Vedic Numerology:

In Vedic system, the planet Neptune was not there at all. The ancients associated Saturn with the Number 7. Thus, the gemstone for planet Saturn is for number 7 people. The Gemstone is Blue Sapphire and is a powerful stone. Even the ancient Numerology based Yantra for Saturn has 7 as basic number in it.

12	7	14
13	11	9
8	15	10

Saturn's Yantra

NUMBER 8

Western Numerology:

Number 8 is the symbol of Saturn in numerology. All those persons born on 8th, 17th, and 26th of a month have number 8 as their number. Those born between 26th January to February 19th-26th have pronounced number 8 qualities.

The main quality of these people is that they are lonely at heart and very intensely at that. They are often misunderstood in life and this leads to melancholy. They are very deep individuals and have the capacity to play a very important role in life. They can become fanatics if they are religious. No argument or opposition can convince them about their fanaticism and they carry out this despite this. This leads to very strong and bitter lifelong enmities for them.

These people have a countenance of a cold and undemonstrative person. But they have very soft and warm feelings for downtrodden and oppressed. They do not make an effort to change the views of people about them. They can be either successful or total failures.

If these people have leanings and aspire then they generally aim for government or public life and hold very high positions in this field. They are ready to sacrifice a lot to serve in such high positions, which allows them to do something for the oppressed. This is not a fortunate number as such and very difficult to explain.

One side of their nature represents great upheaval, revolution, anarchy and all kinds of kinky thought and eccentricities. But the other side of nature is deeply philosophical, leaning for occult and deep studies, zeal for certain causes. They feel that they are different and their virtues are generally recognized after their death.

These people of number 8 should carry out major activities on a date with number 8 as its root. Their lucky day is Saturday. They get connected to number 4 people also and thus Sunday and Monday are good days for them also. Their lucky colours are dark gray, dark blue and purple. Light colours make them look different and out of synchronous with those clothes.

Their lucky stones are Amethyst and Dark Sapphire, Black Pearl and black diamond also suits them. These stones give them the depth, which they feel very comfortable with. They should wear Dark Sapphire if possible all the time.

Vedic Numerology;

The Vedic system of numerology associates Rahu with the number 8. Thus Hessonite becomes the stone for number 8 people. The ancient Numerological Yantra for Rahu has 8 as basic number as below.

13	8	15
14	12	10
9	16	11

Rahu's Yantra

NUMBER 9

Western Numerology:

The number of Mars is number 9. All persons born on 9th, 18th or 27th of a month are number 9 people. But they get pronounced number 9 qualities if they are born between 21st March to April 19th-26th or during 21st October to November 20th-27th.

The main quality of number 9 persons is that they have warrior like attitude. They fight till the end for any issue. The will power is very high in them. They generally struggle in early part of life but in the end they succeed due to the determination and will power they possess. They are very hasty and impulsive by nature. They do not want to be lorded over but want to be their own masters. Since they have great courage, they are excellent soldiers and leaders with perseverance.

The major drawback for them is hastiness and the concomitant foolhardiness. They have tendency to suffer due to fire and explosions also. They also undergo operations in life more than people born under other numbers. They also suffer quarrels and strife at home or with their relations in life. They resent criticism and do not like to be looked down upon. They would rather be leaders and looked up to. Their managerial abilities are excellent but it only works if they are given free hands. They are good administrators as they have a subtle ruthlessness about them. If interfered with, then they do not get indulgence and do not put an effort to set things right which they perceive have gone wrong due to interference even at the cost of everything getting ruined.

They get along with persons of number 9 very easily and also get along with 3 and 6 number people. 9 is a lucky number to be born but the temper and the vibrations are overwhelming. If these are controlled and channelised, then remarkable success can be achieved by 9 number persons. These persons should carry out their plans on those dates, which come to 9 number. Their lucky days are Tuesdays, Thursday and Friday.

Their gemstones are Ruby, Garnet and bloodstone. They should wear one all their life.

Vedic Numerology:

In Vedic system of numerology, the number 9 is associated with Ketu. Ketu's gemstone is Cat's eye and is very suitable for number 9 people. The ancient numerological Yantra for Ketu has 9 as the basic number in it as below.

14	9	16
15	13	11
10	17	12

Ketu's Yantra

Chapter 13

Case Studies

Here we will discuss some cases where the principles explained in the book have been utilized while recommending gemstones to people. These cases have been taken from the databank of the author, which is being collected from people actually coming for advice.

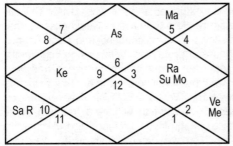

Case-1

This is the case of a person who runs his own consultancy company and had contacted as he was facing some professional problems. He was trying to open a new company and was facing obstacles. He was running Mercury-Ketu dasa. In his chart Ketu is placed in 4th house thus causing him problems in personal family life. When probed he came out with the fact that he was also having problems with his wife and the situation had reached almost breaking point.

He was advised to wear an Emerald immediately and since his dasa was about to change from Mercury-Ketu to Mercury- Venus, I advised him to wait for the right time to come and go into one of the options to open a company which deals with glamour. The stone worked very well for him and in Jan 2005 he has opened the company and is getting top clients for the company. His communication skills are showing results and the feedback has been very positive.

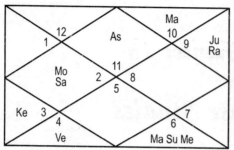

Case-2

This is the chart of a lady who contacted the author for seeking advice on professional front. She had been facing stagnation and was not feeling fully satisfied with her work profile. She is running Rahu-Sun dasa. 7th lord Sun in 6th house with 10th lord Mars and 8th lord Mercury makes her lot of effort. Rahu is well placed and she was advised to wear a Diamond for luck and prosperity. Here the readers would observe that Mars in 8th house does not allows us to recommend Red Coral for her, though Mars is lord of 10th house of profession. Venus being Yogakaraka planet in her chart would give her some health problems and with Diamond it may further aggravate but it will help her in her luck favouring her as well. It should be seen that Venus and Moon have exchanged houses and actually makes a yoga which will help her win some competitive situation in the dasa of Rahu-Moon. Diamond also will enhance that factor being in 6th house. Moreover, Venus exalts in her Navamsa chart indicating that Diamond will not harm her if worn.

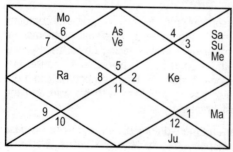

Case-3

This is the chart of a lady who is now a senior HR executive in a multinational company in Bangalore. She had been trying to change her job as she was also facing stagnation in her job in Jan 2003 when she contacted the author.

Look at the horoscope. She was running Rahu-Mars at that time. Though her job was good and well paying but 6:8 relation of Rahu Mars indicates problems. Sun Saturn conjunction also shows problems with boss. That was exactly the problem and she wanted to change the job. Look at Jupiter. It is 5th and 8th lord placed in 8th house and it is also Vargottam. Her Jupiter dasa was to begin in March 2003. I asked her to wear a Yellow Sapphire and told her to be patient till March.

She got a top job in the company where she presently works and her profile is constantly changing. Now she has also shifted to Bangalore also and many other predictions were given to her which are yet to happen.

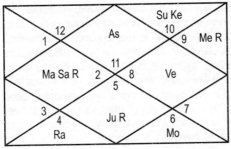

Case-4

This is the case of a entrepreneur who is mired in a number of court cases related to his business and had a successful life abroad. His businesses in India and abroad are almost closed and is trying to rebuild his life so that he is able to clear his debts.

His horoscope shows that in Saturn period he will have problems in his profession as it aspects the 10th house and is afflicting the 10th lord as well. He is running dasa of Saturn –Venus when he contacted the author. He wanted to know about resurrecting his business. Saturn Venus period should give him some respite and he may start his business. He was advised to wear a Diamond immediately. Venus being yogakaraka planet for him and in 10th house, Diamond will help him. Now in Feb 2005, he contacted again and told that starting a business again is in sight and he is having final negotiations with some people to start business in Madhya Pradesh.

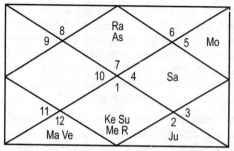

Case-5

This is the case of a lady who contacted the author about her career issues. Look at the horoscope. She was running dasa of Sun-Ketu at the time when she contacted. Sun is exalted and is very strong in Dasamsa chart but is with Saturn in Dasamsa. Ketu is afflicting Sun. This indicates some frustrations in any activity she was doing. When probed further, she admitted that she was very anxious about her marriage. This cleared up my interpretation of her chart. The dasa period is focussed in 7th house and this anxiety about married life was a clear indication. Her career issues were actually secondary. I advised her to wear a Blue Sapphire for career benefits. Saturn being Yogakaraka for her is placed in 10th house. She is doing very well in her career and other techniques of propitiation for dasa period have also helped her immensely.

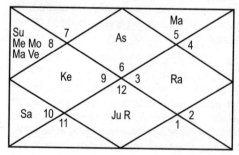

Case-6

This case is of a wife of senior IAS officer. She herself is a pathologist and had lot of problems. She contacted as she was having many health problems and felt very low due to this.

Look at the chart. Moon and Venus are both afflicted by Mars and Venus is conjunct Mars in 8th house of her Navamsa chart. It came out true that she had problems of menstrual systems which is clear in Navamsa chart. She was advised to wear an Emerald as it is the lagna lord and will help her physical being. She was also prescribed other remedial measures for the running dasa of Venus-Venus. After one year, she has given the feedback of having improved dramatically and feels surprised being a doctor herself.

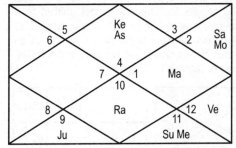

Case-7

This case belongs to a lady who contacted the author for knowing about her personal life. She wanted to know about her career change in the context of personal life. The look at the chart shows that 7th house is afflicted by Rahu-Ketu axis. She was running dasa of Rahu. 4th house is aspected by Mars. This also affects domestic happiness.

She was running Rahu-Venus and Venus is exalted. She was asked to wear a Red Coral as it is yogakaraka and is very nicely placed in 10th house of Navamsa also. After wearing the stone, she suddenly told me one day that she has got an offer for shifting to a new company. She quit her job and started working with upstart company. After 2 months, she has done a very good business in this period. Mars being 10th lord and very strong would give her a good career all through as it is nicely placed in Navamsa chart and Dasamsa chart as well.

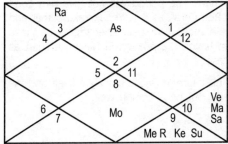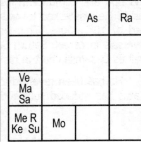

Case-8

This is the chart of a very senior IAS officer colleague. He wanted to know about his career in general from me. He was running the dasa of Venus-Venus. Look at the horoscope. Venus is lagna lord and is afflicted by Saturn and Mars in 9th house. Placement is fine but affliction is heavy. Venus is 6th lord as well.

Since his Venus dasa had started, I asked him to wear Diamond, which he did. This gave good results to him and he got shifted to a better position in his job where he was happy but overworked. This also gave benefits in terms of his wife's health. See that Venus as Karaka of Wife is heavily afflicted. Venus dasa gave his wife health frailty, which did improve after he wore Diamond.

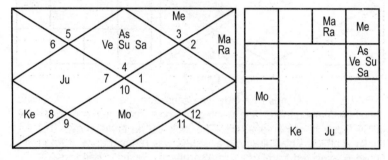

Case-9

The case is also of a senior officer of Government of India. He occupied the adjacent room to the author's room in office. He wanted to know about his career again as he was expecting changes which may have marred his growth.

Look at his chart. He was running Saturn-Venus period when he contacted. Saturn – Sun would start in December 2004. I told him to face some reversal from government as soon as Saturn-Sun starts. Saturn and Sun are Conjunct in his chart. The period will not give him good result. He was asked to wear Red Coral, as it is Yogakaraka planet and lord of 10th house. This would make him bear the effects of these reversals in career. Saturn Sun have 2:12 relation in Navamsa chart as well as Dasamsa chart in his case.

He has been reverted to his cadre in December 2004 itself and the status has reduced substantially. But he is coping well.

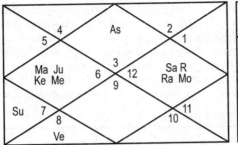

Case-10

This is the case of a lady who is wife of a colleague IAS officer. The lady wanted to know about her depressive state of mind extending upto suicidal tendencies. Look at the chart. She was running Venus-Saturn period. Moon is afflicted by Saturn and Rahu and it is hemmed in between malefics. This also is an eclipse. It shows that she is generally a melancholic person. In the Saturn antardasa, this was manifesting more and she was warned of oncoming Moon pratyantar, that these tendencies will increase. She was asked to wear Pearl and Emerald both and was also asked to do some mantras with Daan also. She gave the feedback in Feb 2005 that she has now come out of that depressive state and enjoys her mantras. The dip in her mental state has passed. In Navamsa, even the Dasa lord is afflicted by Mars and Moon is again afflicted by Saturn.

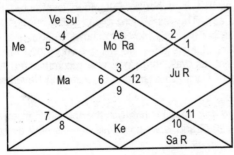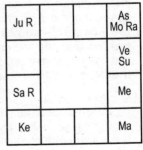

Case-11

This is the chart of another very senior IAS officer colleague. The officer contacted author to know about his next career shift, which was a bit unorthodox.

Look at his chart. He was running Saturn-Mercury dasa. I told him that he will change to the new job due to some compulsion and the status would be downgraded. Mercury is debilitated in Dasamsa chart and in birth chart also is in 3rd house. I told him that he will make efforts also to go for this job, which actually he told me that he was doing. He was asked to wear a Yellow Sapphire. Jupiter is lord of 10th house in 10th house and is exalted in Dasamsa. This would give him protection of career. Blue Sapphire was not recommended because as 8th lord, it may prove bad for him. Moreover, Saturn as a malefic is retrograde and gives more malefic results.

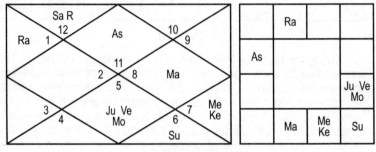

Case-12

This is the case of an executive working with a multinational company. He had been trying to change his job but was not getting it despite going for a number of interviews.

Look at his chart. He was running Moon-Sun period. Moon is 6th lord placed in 7th house with two benefics. But Moon is afflicted in Dasamsa and is debilitated also. Thus as 6th lord it was giving hurdles to him. Sun as 7th lord was in 8th house, which also shows frustrations. I told him that with the onset of Mars dasa, he will get very good offer and will join a very good job as well. Red Coral was recommended to him. Mars is in 10th house of Dasamsa chart and is exalted in Navamsa also.

The feedback he gave was that he has got the job offer from a good company in January, 2005 and is weighing his options now as he is awaiting of other interviews as well.

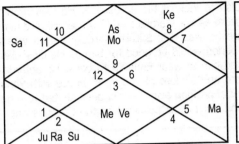

Case-13

The above case is of another IAS officer colleague. He had a bad married life, which ended in divorce. He wanted to know about his future personal life.

Look at his chart. 7th lord Mercury is well placed and has no affliction. But in Navamsa chart, Mercury is afflicted by Saturn in 12th house. In Bhava chart Mercury shifts to 6th house and joins Sun. 7th house in Navamsa is aspected by Mars. Moreover, he was running the period of Moon, which is 8th lord in his chart and is afflicted by Saturn in Navamsa chart. This shows his troublesome married life.

When he contacted the author, he was running Moon-Sun period. Mars dasa can bring hope, he was told. Mars aspects 7th house in Navamsa where Jupiter is placed. He was recommended Yellow Sapphire as it is lagna lord and 4th lord and will help him derive family happiness and get married. The feedback came after 2 months that he has got a match for marriage again and may get married in middle of 2005.

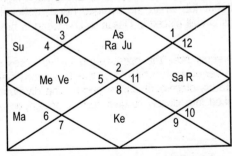

Case-14

This is the chart of a senior IPS officer. He being a close friend of the author met him and he was wearing Blue Sapphire already recommended by some astrologer.

He asked author also to look at his horoscope. He was running Saturn-Saturn period. Saturn as Yogakaraka in 10th house will give him a very top position, where he was. His Saturn-Mercury period was to start in Nov. 2004. The period would be good for him as Mercury exalts in Dasamsa chart. I asked him to wear Emerald to boost his antardasa period. Mercury is 2nd lord and 5th lord placed in 4th house with Venus. This will help in his financial position also. He has been shifted to a new job, which is equally good but not as powerful as the previous one.

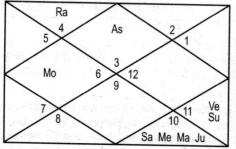

Case-15

This is the case of an Indian Information Service Officer. He was reverted to his own parent cadre and got demoted. He was trying to get a position where, he would avoid demotion.

Look at the chart. He was running Jupiter–Ketu period. Jupiter as 10th lord is placed in 8th house debilitated but getting Neechbhanga. Jupiter is placed in 8th house of Navamsa chart but is in 9th house of Navamsa chart. I asked him to wear Yellow Sapphire, as Jupiter is lagna lord. He was able to get that job where he avoided his demotion in Jupiter-Venus period. Venus is well placed in Dasamsa chart and in birth chart as well.

The above examples show how the prescription in live cases is done. The factors, which require attention, are the Dasa lord and antardasa lord and their status, placement and strength. The divisional charts also need to be looked into closely to give correct prescriptions.